THE DAD DIARIES

Gluten-Free

Family Adventures

JOSEPH TITO

ISBN: 978-1-0690946-3-6

www.thedaddiaries.com

To Stella and Mia, my incredible little whirlwinds of joy—you never stop asking questions, and honestly, sometimes I'm just making up the answers. But your giggles, your wonder, and the way you look at the world like it's one giant playground? That stuff inspires me every single day. This book's for you.

To Frank, my partner in crime—seriously, you're the one who keeps me sane when I'm knee-deep in flour or questioning my life choices over a pot of burnt soup. I couldn't have pulled this off without your endless supply of hugs, patience, and really good takeout recommendations. You're my rock, my chef-in-training, and sometimes, let's be real, my sous-chef-slash-dishwasher.

To my parents—you guys showed me that good food doesn't just taste amazing; it's a love language. You taught me how to properly season everything (and not just with salt), and more importantly, you showed me that family meals are where all the magic happens. This book exists because of everything you passed down. Also, sorry for all those times I "helped" in the kitchen and made a giant mess. I was... learning.

And to all the parents out there—whether you're crushing it or just trying to get through dinner without someone throwing a tantrum (and let's be honest, it's not always the kids), I hope this book brings some laughs, a little less stress, and a lot more flavour to your crazy, beautiful ride.

Joseph Tito

@thedaddiaries.ca

Meet Joseph Tito, the powerhouse behind "The Dad Diaries." Forget any preconceived notions of a typical dad because Joseph is anything but. Living it up in Toronto, he's redefining the dad game as a parenting influencer with a serious knack for finding the funny in the chaos of fatherhood. With his hands full raising 5-year-old twin girls, Joseph isn't just surviving the wild ride of parenting—he's turning it into entertainment.

But Joseph's talents don't stop at making people laugh. He's also an accomplished author. His children's book, "The Twin Diaries: Stella and Mia Meet Papa," captures the hearts of kids and parents alike, while his deeply personal memoir, "From Jet-Setter to Fatherhood," dives into his transformative journey through surrogacy. These aren't just books; they're windows into the soul of a man who's tackled life's curveballs with grace and humour.

Now, let's talk about his kitchen skills. Joseph invites you to join him in culinary adventures that promise more than just a meal. Dive into his world of family-friendly, gluten-free cuisine that's as delightful as his anecdotes. So, strap in and get ready for some real talk, hearty laughs, and damn good food. Joseph isn't just dishing out recipes; he's serving up slices of life, seasoned with a healthy dose of reality and a pinch of salt.

Table of Contents

Introduction

Hey there, fellow parents, kitchen adventurers, and non-cooks like me! I'm Joseph Tito, the guy behind The Dad Diaries, and if you're holding this book, you probably have a thing or two in common with me: a career that keeps you on your toes, the joyful chaos of twin 4-year-olds, and a knack for needing meals that appear as fast as your kids' attention spans.

But before we dive into the world of quick and easy gluten-free recipes, let me share a little secret with you—a secret that led me down this culinary path in the first place. You see, I've had a lifelong struggle with gut health issues. It wasn't the most glamorous part of my life, but it was undoubtedly one of the most influential in shaping the direction of this book.

From a young age, I was plagued by digestive discomfort, bloating, and a general feeling of unwellness. It was as if my stomach had a mind of its own, and it wasn't particularly friendly. I knew something was amiss, but my initial attempts at finding answers left me with more questions than solutions.

I travelled the globe seeking medical advice, consulting specialists, gastroenterologists, and naturopaths. I underwent countless tests, from blood work to endoscopies, and they all had one thing in common—they confirmed that I was, according to medical standards, perfectly healthy.

Yet, my stomach begged to differ. It was a constant companion, and not in a good way. No amount of gym visits or attempts at eating healthier seemed to make it go away. The endless bloating and discomfort left me searching for answers. And after consulting with specialists, naturopaths, and gut health experts, I received a diagnosis that sent shockwaves through my Italian heritage—I needed to go gluten-free.

Now, if you've ever known an Italian, you'll understand that this is no small revelation. Italians, myself included, have an undying love affair with pasta, pizza, and all things gluten. So, when I heard the words "gluten-free," it was like telling a fish to live without water. But sometimes, life throws you a curveball, and you've got to learn to swing with it.

I faced a choice: cling to tradition, hold on to my beloved gluten-rich dishes, and continue suffering in silence, or embark on a journey toward better health. As a father and husband, the decision was clear—I needed to prioritize my family's well-being.

So, there I was, standing at the crossroads of tradition and health, with my twin daughters looking up to me for guidance. I knew it wouldn't be easy, but I had a mission—to make this gluten-free journey not just bearable but enjoyable for my family. And so, my culinary adventure began.

My kitchen transformed into a laboratory of experimentation, where I would test and tweak recipes to create gluten-free dishes that rivalled their gluten-filled counterparts. I embarked on a quest to find the perfect balance between health and taste, to prove that gluten-free didn't mean sacrificing flavour and enjoyment.

My twin daughters, my most discerning critics, became my sous chefs, my taste-testers, and my biggest motivators. Their honest opinions and delighted smiles, when they tasted my creations, fuelled my determination.

Together, we discovered a world of gluten-free possibilities that went far beyond the traditional Italian fare. We explored the richness of gluten-free grains like quinoa and rice, the versatility of nut flours, and the magic of gluten-free oats. We uncovered the hidden treasures of gluten-free sauces and seasonings that could turn ordinary meals into extraordinary ones.

Our kitchen became a place of bonding, laughter, and learning. We shared stories, made memories, and celebrated each culinary triumph, no matter how small. My daughters learned the joys of cooking, and I learned the immeasurable value of quality time spent with loved ones.

Through this journey, I discovered that gluten-free cooking wasn't a limitation but an invitation to creativity. It was a chance to explore new ingredients, experiment with unique combinations, and surprise our taste buds with unexpected delights.

And so, this cookbook was born—not out of the desire to become a gourmet chef, but out of the need to create simple, delectable, and gluten-free dishes that would nourish my family's bodies and spirits. If you've ever found yourself in a similar predicament, torn between health and tradition, you're not alone. This book is for you.

Throughout these pages, I'll share the recipes that have become staples in my home. They're the dishes that have brought joy back to our family meals, proving that you don't need a pantry full of gluten to enjoy the pleasures of the kitchen. Together, we'll explore a world of flavours that cater to busy lives, demanding careers, and the ever-present chaos of parenting.

But enough chatter from me; it's time to roll up those sleeves and get cooking. So grab your apron (or superhero cape if you're anything like my twins), and let's dive into the beautiful world of gluten-free, kid-approved cuisine. Welcome to The Dad Diaries gluten-free adventures—it's going to be a tasty and hilarious ride!

As we embark on this culinary adventure, remember it's not just about the food; it's about the laughter, the memories, and the joy that comes with sharing a meal with loved ones. So, let's turn our kitchens into the heart of our homes and let the cooking begin!

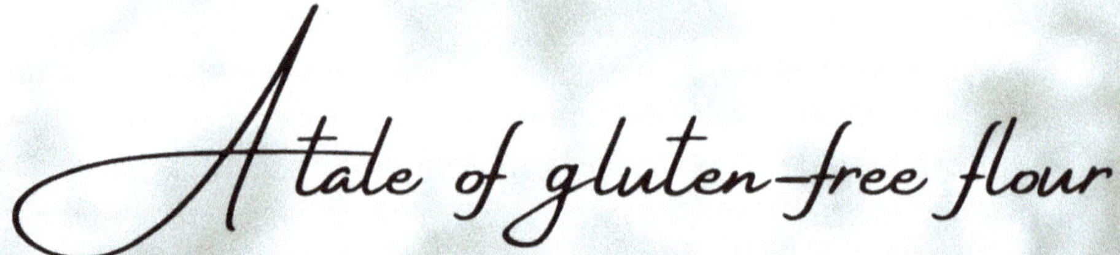

A tale of gluten-free flour

A lot of my recipes call for flour, so let's explore the fascinating world of gluten-free flour. If you're navigating the realm of gluten-free cooking, you'll soon discover that there's a whole family of flours waiting to be your trusty sidekick in the kitchen. Each one has its unique personality, just like our kids do, and they're ready to make your gluten-free dishes shine.

1. **Almond Flour** - The Nutty Sidekick

Imagine your dependable sidekick, the almond. Almond flour is like that loyal friend who always has your back. Made from ground, blanched almonds (sans the skins), it boasts a nutty flavour that's perfect for all your baking endeavours. Plus, it's packed with minerals like iron, magnesium, and vitamin E. However, it's a bit of a calorie champ, with 640 calories per cup—200 more than wheat flour! While almonds themselves are gluten-free, always check the label to ensure your almond flour hasn't mingled with gluten.

2. **Buckwheat Flour** - The Earthy Rebel

Buckwheat, despite the misleading name, is the rebel of the family. It's not wheat; it's a pseudocereal! Buckwheat flour adds an earthy twist to your recipes and is ideal for quick breads. But be forewarned, it's crumbly by nature. To make it shine, mix it with other gluten-free flour, like brown rice flour. It's high in B-vitamins, iron, and antioxidants, including the anti-inflammatory polyphenol rutin. But remember, cross-contamination is a possibility, so opt for certified gluten-free buckwheat flour.

3. **Sorghum Flour** - The Ancient Sage

Sorghum flour, our ancient sage, has been around for over 5,000 years. Naturally gluten-free and the fifth most important cereal grain globally, it adds a mild, sweet flavour to your dishes. It's a dense flour, perfect for blending with other gluten-free flours or when you need just a touch. Sorghum is a powerhouse of fibre, protein, and iron. It also carries antioxidants to help you combat inflammation. Yet, tread carefully; sorghum flour may encounter gluten during processing, so always look for that certified gluten-free label.

4. **Amaranth Flour** - The Nutrient Ninja

Amaranth is the ninja of gluten-free flours. This pseudocereal can stealthily replace up to 25% of wheat flour, lending your creations an earthy, nutty taste. It's brimming with fibre, protein, and a slew of essential micronutrients, including manganese, magnesium, and iron. These nutrients are your allies in supporting brain health, bone strength, and DNA synthesis. But beware, gluten contamination might lurk if amaranth is processed near its gluten-rich buddies.

5. **Teff Flour** - The Mighty Mite

Teff, the smallest grain on the planet, packs a mighty punch. It comes in various hues, from mild to earthy, and is famous for making Ethiopian injera bread. Now, it's also making waves in pancakes, cereals, and more. Substituting 25-50% of wheat or all-purpose flour with teff flour brings in not only that distinct flavour but also high protein, calcium, and vitamin C – a rare find in ancient grains. For a gluten-free dad's peace of mind, always check the processing label.

6. **Arrowroot Flour** - The Versatile Wonder

Arrowroot flour is the jack-of-all-trades in the gluten-free flour family. Derived from a tropical plant, it thickens soups, sauces, and pies without a distinct taste. It partners well with almond, coconut, or tapioca flours to create crunchy or crispy delights. It might even provide a subtle immune boost, packed with potassium, B-vitamins, and iron. Your secret weapon for culinary success, dads!

7. **Brown Rice Flour** - The Nutty Neighbor

Brown rice flour, your friendly neighbour in the gluten-free world. It contains the whole grain, providing fibre and essential nutrients like protein, magnesium, and iron. Its nutty essence makes it ideal for roux, breading, or even baked goods like cookies and cakes. But here's the catch – rice flour can be prone to gluten contamination during processing. So, ensure your brown rice flour had a safe journey.

8. **Oat Flour** - The Heart-Healthy Hero

Oat flour, the heart-healthy hero, offers more flavour than regular flour and a chewy, crumbly texture. Baking with oat flour can make your dishes moister and even lower "bad" LDL cholesterol, blood sugar, and insulin levels, thanks to beta-glucan, a soluble fibre. It's a treasure trove of nutrients, including protein, magnesium, phosphorus, B-vitamins, and antioxidants. But there's a caveat. Gluten contamination is possible based on where and how the oats are processed. To keep your recipes truly gluten-free, look for certified gluten-free oat flour.

9. **Corn Flour** - The Eye Health Guardian

Corn flour, made from finely ground cornmeal, is a common thickener and a key player in tortillas and bread. It comes in white and yellow varieties and can blend seamlessly with other gluten-free flours to craft the perfect pizza crust. It's rich in fibre and brimming with carotenoids like lutein and zeaxanthin, which work wonders for your eyes, reducing the risk of cataracts and age-related macular degeneration. It also serves up a hearty portion of vitamin B6, thiamine, manganese, and magnesium. Yet, cross-contamination risks are higher in processed foods, so stay vigilant, dads!

10. **Chickpea Flour** - The Legume Lover

Chickpea flour, derived from the versatile chickpea, offers a nutty, grainy texture. It's a star in Middle Eastern and Indian cuisine, creating falafel, hummus, and the flatbread socca. Packed with fibre and plant-based protein, it's the duo that slows digestion, keeps you full, and manages body weight. And there's more; chickpea flour delivers a heart-boosting combo of magnesium and potassium. Yet, beware of those pesky traces of gluten from cross-contamination in certain manufactured foods.

11. **Coconut Flour** - The Tropical Treat

Coconut flour is the tropical treat that brings a hint of the exotic to your baking. With its light texture and mild coconut flavour, it's perfect for bread and desserts. But here's the trick: coconut flour soaks up more water than other flours, so be ready to adjust your recipe accordingly. It's rich in lauric acid, a medium-chain triglyceride that provides energy and may also team up with its fibre content to lower "bad" LDL cholesterol. It's a saviour for those with nut and gluten allergies, but be vigilant – contamination can happen during processing.

12. **Tapioca Flour** - The Immune Booster

Tapioca flour is a thickener extracted from the South American cassava root. It's a chameleon with no discernible taste and can be your secret weapon in thickening soups, sauces, and pies or joining the league of gluten-free flour in bread recipes. While it might not be a nutritional powerhouse, it has one ace up its sleeve – resistant starch. This starch functions like fibre, improving insulin sensitivity, lowering blood sugar levels, and even curbing your appetite. Just remember to avoid mixing it with gluten-containing flour if you're on a gluten-free mission.

13. **Cassava Flour** - The Culinary Chameleon

Cassava flour, the culinary chameleon, hails from South America and is the counterpart to tapioca flour. It resembles white flour and easily slides into recipes that call for all-purpose flour. It's a neutral-flavoured, easily digestible option that's lower in calories compared to coconut or almond flours. Cassava flour also carries the precious gift of resistant starch, which is linked to lowering blood sugar levels and improving insulin sensitivity. Although processing the cassava root might reduce its resistant starch content, you can trust that cassava flour is less likely to play host to gluten. Still, keep an eye on where it was processed.

14. **Tigernut Flour** - The Sweet Specialist

Tigernut flour, despite its name, isn't a nut. It's made from small root vegetables that thrive in North Africa and the Mediterranean. It's your go-to choice for baked goods with a sweet and nutty flavour. The bonus? Its natural sweetness lets you dial down the sugar. It's a tad coarser than white flour, adding texture to your culinary creations. A mere quarter-cup of tigernut flour packs 10 grams of fibre, which helps in lowering cholesterol. Plus, it's rich in healthy monounsaturated fat, iron, phosphorus, potassium, and vitamins E and C.

1**5. Millet** - The Delicate Dandy

With its mild sweetness, Millet delicately contributes volume and texture to baked goods. If you're making bread, rolls, or any kind of baked delight, consider millet as your sidekick. It's a well-rounded addition to your gluten-free kitchen with 4 grams of protein, 1 gram of fibre, 2 grams of fat, 31 grams of carbohydrates, and 150 calories per quarter cup.

16. Potato - The Moisture Maestro

Potato flour, the moisture maestro, holds the secret to making your yeast bread recipes a hit. At 20% of the total flour, it improves the aroma, texture, and flavour of flatbreads, delivering that perfect balance of moisture and structure. It's also a star thickener for gravies, sauces, and soups. But remember, there's another player in the game – potato starch. It's a potent substitute for cornstarch and can withstand higher cooking temperatures, adding moisture to your baked goods. So, if you're planning to whip up a gluten-free cake flour blend, think rice and a touch of potato or tapioca.

These gluten-free flours are your allies in the kitchen, each with its own superpower. You'll need to fine-tune your recipes and be diligent about potential cross-contamination, but with the right flour by your side, you can conquer the gluten-free world one delicious dish at a time. So, put on your apron, gather your ingredients, and let's start cooking up a storm!

All-Purpose Flour: My go-to when I'm in the kitchen whipping up something delicious is Caputo Fioreglut. It's like the hidden treasure chest for gluten-free pizza and bread lovers. This little secret comes all the way from Italy, and you can snag it on Amazon or, if you're lucky, at your local grocery store.

Now, what makes Caputo Flour the superhero of gluten-free flour? It's super fine, so you won't have any of that annoying gritty texture ruining your culinary masterpiece. But here's the catch – it contains gluten-free wheat starch. So, if you're in the "no-wheat club," steer clear of this one, my friends.

But hey, if you can't find Caputo Flour or you're up for a bit of kitchen adventure, I've got you covered with a DIY gluten-free flour mix. It's like making your own superhero team for baking. Here's the recipe for 5 cups of flour:

- 285g of Potato Starch
- 250g of White Rice Flour
- 75g of Tapioca Starch/Flour
- 75g of Whey Protein Isolate
- 15g of Xanthan Gum

This mix right here is your ticket to gluten-free baking glory. So, whether you go for the Italian magic of Caputo or decide to create your own flour dream team, just remember, the kitchen is your kingdom, and you're the ruler of the flour!

Ah, breakfast. That glorious time of day when our adorable little human alarm clocks—also known as our kids—wake us up before the sun even has a chance. There they are, bouncing off the walls with boundless energy while we're stumbling around the kitchen like zombies, desperately trying to locate the coffee maker without actually opening our eyes. Somehow, they seem to think 5 a.m. is prime time for deep philosophical discussions or requesting pancakes shaped like their favorite cartoon character. And here we are, just trying to remember how spoons work.

But hey, fear not, fellow sleep-deprived heroes! This chapter is your guide to turning that breakfast chaos into something that vaguely resembles order—or at least a version of it where everyone gets fed and no one cries (too much). We're here to tackle the breakfast battle head-on, with recipes that might just make the pickiest eater pause in their protest, and make even the most exhausted parent feel like they've got this. Yes, even if you've already had to break up a pre-dawn fight over who gets the blue bowl before you've had your first life-saving sip of coffee.

And listen, it's okay if breakfast doesn't look perfect. In my house, some mornings are about flipping golden-brown pancakes while Stella sneaks extra chocolate chips into the batter, insisting it's "for good luck." Other mornings, it's about realizing there's no milk and improvising cereal with orange juice—yes, we've tried that, and no, I don't recommend it. But what I've learned through all these mornings, both the messy and the magical, is that it's not really about the perfect breakfast spread. It's about the little smiles, the moments when Mia insists on sitting in my lap to eat because "it tastes better that way," and the laughter when we realize we've mixed up the salt and sugar. Again.

So, let's suit up (or just throw on whatever isn't covered in yesterday's dinner) and get to it. We're going to flip, scramble, and bake our way through the morning madness. Grab your spatula, channel your inner sunrise enthusiast, and let's make breakfast a win. Because at the end of the day, getting everyone fed without a meltdown (yours or theirs) is nothing short of morning glory. And whether you're wrangling toddlers, teenagers, or even just yourself, that first meal of the day is worth celebrating—imperfections and all.

Breakfast
the dad diaries

CASSAVA PANCAKES
A breakfast delight

Prepare Time
15 Minutes

Cook Time
4 Minutes

Serves
6 Pancakes

Breakfast is a sacred ritual in many households, and what better way to start your day than with a stack of delicious Cassava Pancakes? These gluten-free wonders are here to make your mornings a little more extraordinary.

Ingredients

- 3/4 cup cassava flour
- 1 1/2 teaspoons baking powder
- 1/2 teaspoon salt
- 1/2 cup canned unsweetened coconut milk
- 1/4 cup water
- 1 egg
- 2 tablespoons pure maple syrup
- 1 tablespoon olive oil

Instructions

1. Grab a medium-sized bowl and whisk together the cassava flour, baking powder, and a pinch of salt. Let the dry ingredients get to know each other.

2. it's time to create the liquid magic in a separate, smaller bowl. Whisk together the coconut milk, water, egg, pure maple syrup, and a dash of olive oil. This is where the pancake charm comes from.

3. Combine the smaller bowl's contents with the larger bowl's dry ingredients. Give it a gentle stir until everything is well-acquainted, but don't overdo it. We want these pancakes to be light and fluffy.

4. Fire up your griddle and lightly oil it to prevent any pancake stickiness. Scoop about 1/4 cup of the batter for each pancake onto the hot griddle. Use the back of your spoon to spread the batter if needed.

5. Cook the pancakes over medium heat for about 2 to 3 minutes on each side. They're ready to flip when you see those bubbles on the surface, and the edges are starting to get that delightful dryness. The result? Golden-brown, fluffy pancakes that are impossible to resist.

6. Once they're cooked to perfection, serve these Cassava Pancakes while they're warm. And don't forget to drizzle a little extra maple syrup on top – because there's no such thing as too much syrup!

These gluten-free Cassava Pancakes are a breakfast treat that's sure to put a smile on your face. I'd love for you to share your stack of pancake perfection with me by tagging @thedaddiaries.ca on Instagram – let's spread the breakfast joy!

Chocolate Chip Pancakes

Sunday mornings are a cherished tradition in our household, a delightful journey into the realm of culinary excellence. At the heart of this weekly ritual are our "World-Famous" Chocolate Chip Pancakes, where the art of sophistication meets the comfort of home.

As the sun bathes the kitchen in a gentle morning glow, we embark on the ritual of creating these pancakes that have become a symbol of warmth and togetherness. It's not just a breakfast; it's a shared experience, a moment frozen in time when the world slows down, and we savour the simple pleasures of family.

Prepare Time
15 Minutes

Cook Time
4 Minutes

Serves
6 Pancakes

Ingredients

- 125g gluten-free plain flour (because gluten is so last season)
- 1 egg
- 250ml chocolate milk
- 1/2 cup chocolate chips
- Butter, for frying™
- Maple or chocolate syrup (optional – if you feel like being extra, which we always do)

Instructions

1. Start by half-heartedly dumping gluten-free flour into a bowl – because who needs the gluten drama? Create a well in the middle, crack an egg in there, and pour in a quarter of the chocolate milk. Use an electric whisk because we are already parents, and we don't need more manual labour. Mix until it looks like a passable pancake batter – don't strain yourself. Let it rest for 20 minutes or until you can't wait any longer. Throw in the chocolate chips like you're tossing confetti at an Italian wedding.

2. Heat a pan with a knob of butter. Pour a small amount of the batter into the pan – make a feeble attempt to swirl it around because artistry is overrated. Cook until the bottom achieves a golden brown colour – or something close enough. Flip it over and repeat until you've exhausted your minimal effort. Stir the mixture between pancakes – because we're all about efficiency.

3. Gather your stack of pancakes and drizzle some maple syrup on top – or chocolate syrup if you're feeling rebellious, which is about as rebellious as we get before noon. Admire your morning "masterpiece" with a half-smile because, let's be honest, it's just pancakes.

These Chocolate Chip Sunday Pancakes are not just a breakfast; they're a celebration wrapped in each delicious bite. The perfect way to savour the sweetness of a lazy Sunday morning!

The great pancake misadventure...

As I stood in the bustling kitchen, surrounded by pots and pans and a flurry of ingredients, I couldn't help but feel a sense of determination. Today, I was going to teach my six-year-old twins, Mia and Stella, the fine art of pancake making. They were ready and eager, their tiny bodies adorned with aprons that were more splattered with past art projects than culinary triumphs.

"Chefs Mia and Stella," I declared, my voice echoing through the room. "Today, we embark on a culinary journey together!" The girls beamed up at me with excitement shining in their eyes. I could see the seriousness in their expressions as they donned their aprons, taking on the roles of seasoned chefs ready to conquer any challenge.

Despite the chaos and mess that inevitably came with cooking with young children, I couldn't help but feel grateful for this moment. It was a reminder that even in the midst of daily responsibilities and routines, there were precious moments like these that I cherished.

With flour-covered hands and giggles erupting from my little apprentices, we began our journey towards perfectly fluffy pancakes. And within those walls of our busy kitchen, time seemed to stand still as we created memories that would last a lifetime.

Our baking adventure began with the crucial ingredient: flour. I carefully handed each twin a measuring cup, but to them, it was no longer just a simple kitchen tool. In their tiny, excited hands, flour became a prop in a whimsical snow-themed play. "It's a blizzard, Papa!" Stella exclaimed, flinging handfuls of flour into the air with the enthusiasm of a weather presenter during a snowstorm.

Meanwhile, Mia took a different approach and created what she called a 'flour angel' on the kitchen counter. As I stood there amidst our homemade winter wonderland, I couldn't help but question my decision to involve the twins in this experiment. Perhaps I should have just opted for cereal instead.

As we moved on to the eggs, I reminded them to be gentle. But it seemed like a hidden message to see if eggs could fly, and soon they were flying everywhere, leaving a yolk-stained trail. Amongst the chaos, I tried to get out the shells as Mia and Stella giggled like mischievous bandits. Our baking adventure wasn't going as planned, but their laughter made it all worth it.

As we gathered in the kitchen, ready for our Saturday morning pancake tradition, Mia's mischievous grin suggested she had something up her sleeve. And sure enough, as we whipped up the batter and poured it onto the sizzling pan, she reached for the sugar container with a twinkle in her eye. "Let's add a bit more sweetness," she declared mischievously. But by 'bit,' Mia meant enough to make a dentist weep and enough to send our blood sugar levels off the charts.

But that wasn't even the craziest part. Stella, not one to be outdone in any situation, decided to take this culinary caper to the next level. With a devilish gleam in her eye, she grabbed for the bag of chocolate chips and dumped them into the mix, turning our innocent pancakes into a chocoholic's dream.

Cooking these monstrosities turned into a chaotic circus act in my kitchen. Batter was flying everywhere as we attempted to flip and flop our way through cooking these sugar-loaded delights. Pancakes landed on the pan with a satisfying sizzle, while others made unexpected guest appearances on the floor.

After what felt like chaos, we finally sat down at the table to eat our creations. The pancakes were lumpy and overcooked, but still sweet. Despite the mess, there was a sense of accomplishment and pride between us. "We're the best pancake chefs!" Mia laughed, with Stella nodding in agreement, chocolate smeared on her face and overflowing with pride.

Frantically wiping up the chaos - flour, snowy footprints, and escaped chocolate chips taunted me from every corner of the kitchen. It dawned on me then: these moments are the ones that stick. "The Dad Diaries" embraces the messy, unpredictable journey of parenthood, one mishap at a time. Because amidst it all, there is love, joy, and an unbreakable bond. So let the messiness ensue - we'll make unforgettable memories along the way.

Cookie Baked Oatmeal

✓

Prepare Time
15 Minutes

✓

Cook Time
20 Minutes

✓

Serves
4

All right, fellow breakfast enthusiasts, let's dive into something that'll make mornings with the kids a tad less chaotic—Cookie Baked Oatmeal! Trust me, I've been there. Trying to get the little ones fed and out the door can be painful. But fear not; this recipe is your secret weapon. It's quick, dairy-free, and packed with enough yum to make you the breakfast hero.

Ingredients

- 2 cups GF oats
- 2 ripe bananas (the spottier, the better!)
- 4 eggs (because, let's face it, we dads can't function without eggs)
- 1 cup milk of your choosing (I rolled with condensed coconut milk, but you do you)
- A pinch of salt (just a smidge to keep things interesting)
- 1 tsp baking soda (the unsung hero of baking)
- Chocolate chips (because, well, chocolate makes everything better, right?)

Instructions

1. Preheat your oven to 350°F.

2. Grab that blender and toss in the oats, those gloriously spotty bananas, eggs, condensed coconut milk (or your milk of choice), a smidge of salt, and a dash of baking soda. Now, blend like a champ until it's smoother than that one time you got the kids to sleep before 9 PM.

3. Pour that velvety batter into your muffin trays.

4. Now, here's where breakfast dreams come true—sprinkle those chocolate chips. It's the secret to making mornings magical.

5. Slide those trays into the preheated oven and let them do their thing for about 20-25 minutes.

Get ready to reclaim your mornings, one delicious bite at a time. This Gluten and Dairy-free Cookie Baked Oatmeal isn't just a recipe; it's a kid and dad-approved breakfast masterpiece! So, give it a try, and let me know how it scores with your little breakfast critics. It's a breakfast adventure worth savouring, and it might just make you the reigning champ of morning meals!

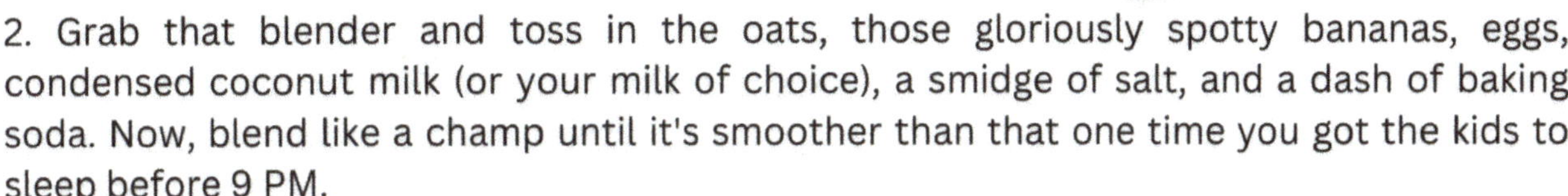

Cinnamon Apple Nut Oatmeal

All right, my dear parents, gather 'round because we're about to create a breakfast masterpiece that'll earn you a standing ovation at the kitchen table. Get ready for Cinnamon Apple Nut Oatmeal - it's like a warm hug for your taste buds, and an added bonus your house will smell like Christmas!

Prepare Time
15 Minutes

Chill Time
15 Minutes

Serves
6

Ingredients

- 2 cups GF large flaked oats (the hearty kind that'll keep you fueled)
- 1 cup cooked apple pieces (you'll need 3-4 apples, but more on that later)
- ½ cup pecans, toasted, roughly chopped (because nuts make everything better)
- ⅓ cup brown sugar (for that sweet morning kickstart)
- 2 tsp ground cinnamon (the spice of life)
- ¼ tsp salt (just a pinch to elevate the flavours)

Instructions for the Apples

1. Grab 3-4 apples, peel 'em, chop 'em up, and toss 'em into a pot of boiling water.

2. Add two tablespoons of cinnamon and two tablespoons of Dark Brown Sugar to the party. Stir it up and let it dance in that boiling water for about 10 minutes. You'll end up with apple perfection!

Instructions

1. In a big ol' bowl, combine those hearty GF large flaked oats, your cinnamon-infused apple pieces, toasted and chopped pecans (because nuts add that satisfying crunch), the brown Sugar (for a hint of caramel goodness), ground cinnamon (because, well, it's the MVP), and a pinch of salt to make those flavours pop. Mix it all up until it's a symphony of ingredients.

2. Stir the oatmeal mixture to make sure all the ingredients are on the same page. Then, pour the contents into a big, heat-proof bowl.

3. Here comes the warmth! Pour in 2 cups of hot oat milk and 1¾ to 2 cups of boiling water. Give it a good stir until everything is playing nicely together. Cover it up with plastic wrap or a lid, and let it chill for 15 minutes.

4. After that well-deserved rest, give it another good stir and portion it out into four bowls.

There you have it, Dad's Cinnamon Apple Nut Oatmeal—a breakfast masterpiece that's as wholesome as it is delicious. Enjoy the warm, cinnamon-infused embrace of this morning treat!

CREAMY COCONUT Quinoa Surprise

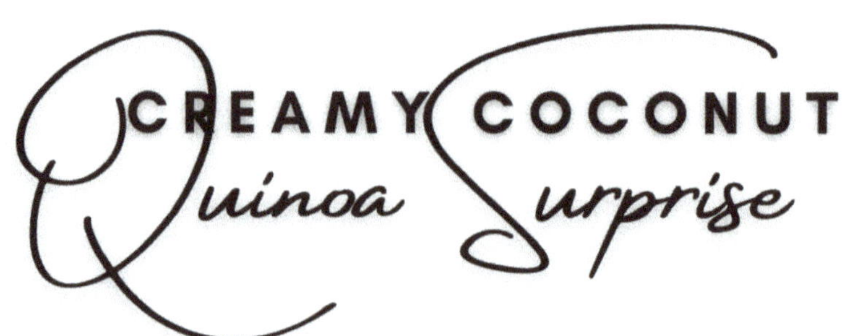

Alright, folks, here's a breakfast that'll make you the hero of the high chair brigade: Creamy Coconut Quinoa Porridge. This isn't just any mushy morning slop; it's a protein-packed powerhouse that'll keep the little tykes full and maybe, just maybe, keep them from bouncing off the walls until lunchtime.

Prepare Time
15 Minutes

Cook Time
40 Minutes

Serves
2

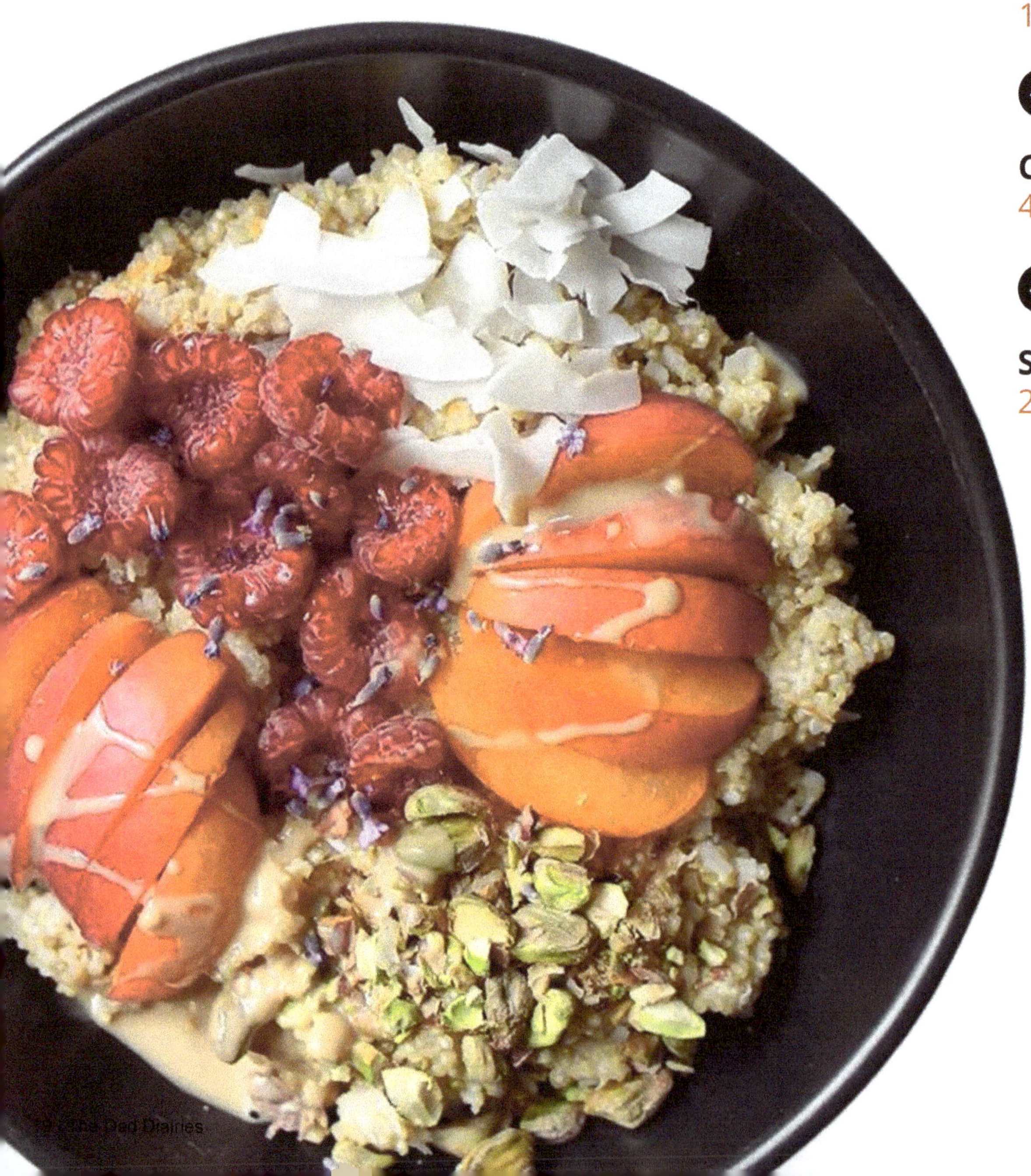

Ingredients

- 1 cup quinoa – Yep, the good stuff that's both kid-approved and secretly healthy.
- 2 cups water
- 2 cups coconut milk – Or whatever milk makes your skirt fly up. Almond, soy, cow… you do you.
- 1/4 cup maple syrup – Because life is bitter enough.
- 1 tsp vanilla extract – For a hint of "What is that yummy taste, Dad?"
- 1/4 tsp salt – Just a pinch to balance the sweet.

Optional

Fresh berries, sliced bananas, chopped nuts, or dried fruit (figs, dates, prunes, sultanas) – Basically, whatever it takes to get them to eat it without a standoff.

Instructions

1. Rinse the quinoa like it's got dirt on it. Because it probably does. Use a fine mesh strainer to avoid accidentally throwing it all down the drain.

2. Dump the rinsed quinoa and water into a medium saucepan. Crank it up to a boil over high heat, then remember you're not in a cooking show and turn it down to low. Slap a lid on it and let it simmer for about 15-20 minutes, or until the quinoa is tender and has sucked up all the water.

3. Once your quinoa is all fluffy and pretentious, stir in the coconut milk, maple syrup, vanilla extract, and that pinch of salt. It's about to smell really good in here, so take a moment to feel like a kitchen wizard.

4. Cover it again and let it simmer for another 10-15 minutes. Keep an eye on it; you want porridge, not a burnt offering. Stir occasionally because, yes, quinoa can and will stick to the bottom if ignored.

5. After the porridge has thickened to your liking (because who am I to judge your porridge preferences), take it off the heat. Let it sit for a few minutes; it's hot and needs to take a breather.

6. Ladle that glorious grain goo into bowls and go to town with the toppings. Make it pretty, make it fun, or just toss it on and call it a day.

And there you have it: a breakfast that's more satisfying than stepping on a Lego. Sit back, watch the magic happen as they devour it, and bask in the glory of starting the morning off right.

Bacon-Kale Frittata

There I was in the Alps, skiing—or at least attempting to without breaking anything. One frosty morning, muscles aching and stomach growling, I stumbled into a cozy mountainside chalet. That's where I found it: the Bacon, Potato, and Kale Frittata. Warm, inviting, and delicious enough to make me forget the cold and my less-than-graceful antics on the slopes. I devoured it, and it was so good, I knew I had to bring this recipe back home. Now, let's dive into how you can recreate this little slice of Alpine heaven, without the risk of skiing mishaps!

Total Time
30 Minutes

Serving
6

Ingredients

- 12 oz tiny red-skin new potatoes, quartered
- 6 slices lower sodium less fat bacon, coarsely chopped
- 2 cups fresh kale, chopped (to pretend we're all about that health life)
- ½ cup coarsely chopped onion (1 medium) (onions, because why not?)
- 8 eggs, lightly beaten (the real MVPs of any frittata)

Instructions

1. In a covered medium saucepan, throw your quartered potatoes into boiling, lightly salted water. Cook them for about 10 minutes, or just until they decide to become tender. Drain and set aside like yesterday's news.

2. While the potatoes are doing their thing, crank up your broiler. Grab a large broiler-proof skillet (because we're about to get serious), and cook that chopped bacon over medium-high heat until it starts to crisp up nicely. This is where things start smelling good.

3. Toss in the kale and onion with the bacon. Cook them for about 5 minutes, or until the onion figures out how to become tender. Stir in those well-behaved potatoes you set aside earlier.

4. In a medium bowl, whisk together the eggs with a dash of hope, 1/4 teaspoon salt, and 1/4 teaspoon ground black pepper. Pour this hopeful mixture over your potato and bacon party. Cook over medium-low heat. As the egg starts setting, get in there with a spatula. Go around the edge of the skillet, lifting the egg mixture so the uncooked bits can sneak underneath. Keep cooking and lifting until the egg is almost set but still looks a bit like it just woke up (surface will be moist).

5. Slide the skillet under the broiler, about 4 to 5 inches from the heat. We're only doing this for 1 to 2 minutes, just until the top decides it's done being wet. If you're more of a baking fan, preheat your oven to 400°F and bake for about 5 minutes, or until it achieves the same dry-top status.

6. Let the frittata take a 5-minute nap. Then slide it onto a serving platter, cut it into six diplomatic wedges, and serve it up like the breakfast champion you are.

There you have it—a frittata that will not only kick-start your morning but also make you feel slightly superior for getting kale and onions into a breakfast dish. Enjoy this slice of Alpine-inspired goodness, and remember, every bite is a taste of a cozy mountainside chalet, right in the comfort of your own kitchen!

Prepare Time
10 Minutes

Cook Time
10 Minutes

Here's a quick culinary adventure for busy parents: Gluten-Free Tortilla Pizzette! It's like a slice of joy on a plate and the ultimate kid-approved treat. These speedy delights are perfect for those days when you need a delicious meal in 15 minutes flat. And it is perfect for a savoury breakfast or pizza party dinner. Just follow along:

- Gluten-free tortillas
- Swiss cheese slices
- Toothpicks (for some culinary magic!)
- Tomato sauce (the saucier, the better)
- Mozzarella cheese (because, let's be honest, can you ever have too much cheese?)
- Prosciutto cotto (fancy ham for the win)
- Protein-packed eggs (for that breakfast-for-dinner vibe)

Instructions

1. Preheat your oven to a toasty 450°F. It's heating up faster than a parent's 'me-time' moment.

2. Grab those gluten-free tortillas, roll up the sides with Swiss cheese, and secure them with toothpicks. It's culinary artistry, folks!

3. Now, slather on that tomato sauce like it's a canvas begging for a saucy masterpiece.

4. Sprinkle on that glorious mozzarella cheese. Go ahead, be generous—cheese rules.

5. Add some prosciutto cotto because fancy ham is the secret ingredient that makes everything better.

6. Time for the grand finale: the protein-packed egg. Crack it right on top of your pizza creation.

7. Pop your culinary masterpiece into the oven and let it bake for a mere 10 minutes. It's quicker than a toddler's attention span.

Voilà! Your Speedy Tortilla Pizzette are ready to steal the spotlight on your breakfast or dinner table. The girls give it two thumbs up! Enjoy these cheesy, gluten-free pizzettes that are bound to make any day feel like a pizza party.

✔ **Prepare Time**
10 Minutes

✔ **Bake Time**
40 Minutes

Introducing a breakfast sensation that'll have you jumping out of bed with excitement—Eggcellent Morning Pizza! This recipe is not just easy; it's a morning game-changer that's perfect for those busy mornings with your little ones. So, let's grab our aprons (or superhero capes, because why not?), and get ready to whip up a breakfast delight that even the pickiest eaters will adore.

Ingredients

- 2 large potatoes, grated
- 2 eggs
- 1/2 cup shredded cheddar cheese
- Salt and pepper, to taste
- 1 cup shredded cheddar cheese (for topping)
- 4 eggs
- Cooked bacon (because everything's better with bacon, right?)

Instructions

1. Preheat your oven to a toasty 400°F. While it's warming up, let's prepare the base of our breakfast pizza. Take those grated potatoes, squeeze them in a dish towel to remove any water and mix them with 2 eggs, 1/2 cup of shredded cheddar cheese, and a pinch of salt and pepper. This is the foundation of our delicious creation.

2. Now, spread this potato and cheese mixture onto a baking sheet, shaping it into a glorious pizza crust. It's like creating a canvas for your breakfast masterpiece.

3. Pop this potato masterpiece into the preheated oven and let it bake for about 20 minutes until it's golden and crispy. Trust me; your kitchen will smell like a breakfast paradise at this point.

4. Once the crust is ready, sprinkle it with a generous helping of cheddar cheese—because can you ever have too much cheese?

5. Crack 4 eggs onto your cheesy canvas, distributing them evenly. This is where the magic happens, as the eggs will bake right into the crust.

6. Now, add some cooked bacon to the mix because, well, bacon makes everything better. Your taste buds will thank you later.

7. Slide your breakfast pizza back into the oven for another 15-20 minutes. This is when the eggs will set, and your pizza will turn into a breakfast work of art.

8. Once it's beautifully golden, take it out, and marvel at your creation. The combination of crispy potato crust, melted cheese, and perfectly baked eggs is a breakfast dream come true.

There you have it, a delightful Breakfast Pizza that's quick, easy, and sure to bring smiles to your breakfast table. So, cut a slice, savour every bite, and start your day with a breakfast that's as satisfying as it is delicious. Enjoy, my fellow breakfast enthusiasts!

Breakfast Casserole

All right, let's talk about morning strategies. As a parent, you know that getting a nutritious breakfast into your kids before they turn into morning monsters is akin to performing a minor miracle. Here's a recipe that's not only kid-approved for its taste but also jam-packed with protein to fuel those little energy machines. This "Dad's Heroic Breakfast Casserole" is your secret weapon to start the day like a champion, featuring a heroic ensemble of hash browns, eggs, and whatever meat scrap you managed to salvage from last night's dinner.

Prepare Time
24 Minutes

Bake Time
40 Minutes

Serving
6

Ingredients

- Nonstick cooking spray (because we'd rather the food stay in their bellies than on the dish)
- 3 cups frozen shredded hash brown potatoes (the real MVPs of any breakfast dish)
- ¾ cup shredded Monterey Jack cheese with jalapeno peppers, or shredded cheddar cheese (because life needs a little spice, or a lot, depending on how late they went to bed)
- 1 cup diced cooked ham, cooked breakfast sausage, or Canadian-style bacon (leftovers are gold)
- ¼ cup sliced green onions (to pretend it's a gourmet dish)
- 4 beaten eggs or 1 cup refrigerated or frozen egg product, thawed (the glue that holds this masterpiece together)
- 1 ½ cups milk, or one 12-ounce can evaporated milk, regular or fat-free (because we all need strong bones)
- ⅛ teaspoon salt
- ⅛ teaspoon black pepper

Instructions

1. Start by spraying a 2-quart square baking dish with nonstick spray like you're defending it from sticky invaders. Lay down a foundation of shredded hash brown potatoes.

2. Sprinkle an even layer of that zesty cheese, your choice of meat, and green onions over the hash browns like you're building the tastiest blanket ever.

3. In a bowl, whip together the eggs, milk, salt, and pepper like you're mixing a potion of invisibility—so the veggies go unnoticed. Pour this magical mixture over the potato pile.

4. Slide that bad boy into a 350°F oven and bake it uncovered for 40-45 minutes. You're aiming for the knife test here—if it comes out clean from the center, you've nailed it.

5. Give it a cool-down break for about 5 minutes; it's been through a lot. Then, cut into servings and watch the disappearance act happen right at your breakfast table.

And there you have it—a breakfast casserole that's almost as heroic as you are on your best dad days. This dish isn't just a meal; it's an easy win in the often-bumpy road of parenting. Serve it up, sit back, and soak in the glory of being the morning hero, even if it's just for today. Here's to conquering the chaos, one protein-packed bite at a time. Enjoy, and remember, each serving comes with a side of peace and quiet (results may vary).

TACO
Egg Cups

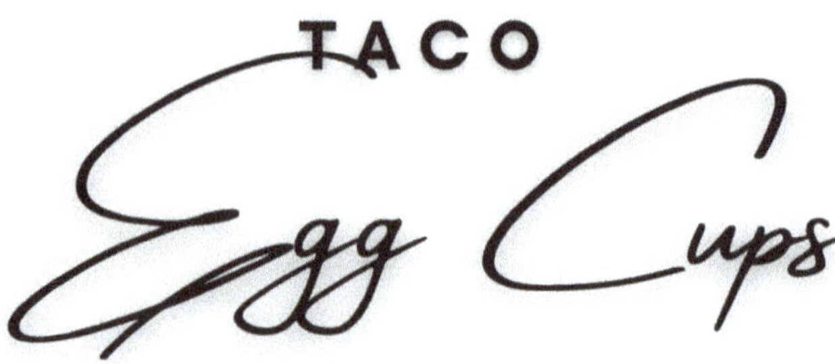

If you're anything like me, you probably believe that breakfast should be a celebration. Well, I've got a bite-sized fiesta for you that will kickstart your day with a burst of flavour. These Taco Egg Cups are not your ordinary breakfast—they're a mini party for your taste buds!

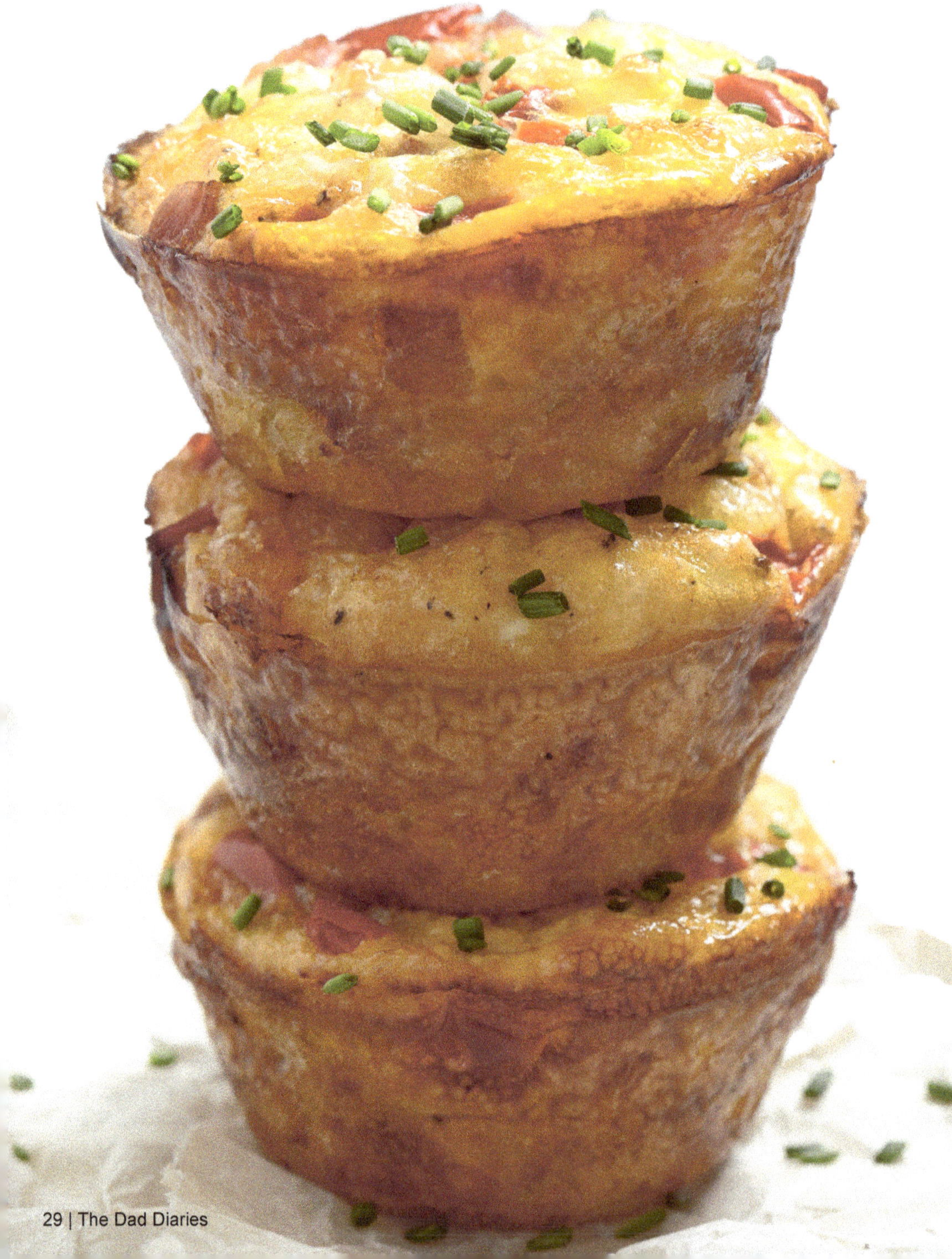

Prepare Time
5 Minutes

Bake Time
18 Minutes

Serves
24 Egg Cups

Ingredients

- 6 eggs
- 3 tablespoons milk
- ½ cup reserved cooked mined meat (seasoned)
- ¼ cup salsa
- 1 cup shredded Cheddar cheese

Instructions

1. Preheat your oven to 350°F and grease a 24-count mini muffin pan. If you're using a regular muffin pan, no worries— just keep an eye on the cooking time (more on that below).

2. In a large bowl, crack those eggs and whisk in the milk until it's a smooth combo.

3. Now, here's where the magic happens. Add your cooked taco meat, salsa, and that glorious shredded Cheddar cheese into the egg mix. Give it a good stir until everything's partying together in the bowl.

4. Spoon this tasty concoction evenly into the muffin pan cups, filling them up to about ¾ full. We're making mini breakfast fiestas, after all!

5. Pop your muffin pan into the preheated oven for 15-18 minutes. You'll know they're ready when the egg cups are set and sport a lovely golden glow on top.

6. Once you see that golden magic, take the pan out of the oven, but hold your horses! Let these mini fiestas cool in the pan for a few minutes.

7. Now, it's the fun part. Carefully remove the Taco Egg Cups from the muffin pan. A small knife or spatula will do the trick.

8. Serve these bite-sized fiestas while they're still warm and get ready to dive into a mini breakfast celebration!

Note: If you're using a regular muffin pan, keep an eagle eye on them while they're in the oven. When they're set and sporting that lovely golden hue, they're ready to rock.

Get ready to savour the mini fiesta, one bite at a time!

Rise and shine with a breakfast that will bring fiesta to your table! Our Breakfast Quesadillas are loaded with mouthwatering flavours and guaranteed to make your morning an adventure. Get the whole family involved as your little chefs create their own quesadilla masterpieces, stuffed with their favourite ingredients. It's a delicious way to start the day and add some magic to your morning routine.

Prepare Time
15 Minutes

Cook Time
10 Minutes

Serves
4

BREAKFAST Quesadillas

 Ingredients

For the Quesadillas:

- Gluten-free tortillas
- 1 cup shredded cheddar cheese (or any cheese you prefer)
- 4 eggs, beaten
- 1 bell pepper, diced
- 1 small onion, diced
- 1/2 cup cooked ham, diced (or substitute with cooked bacon or sausage)
- Olive oil for cooking
- Salt and pepper to taste

For Serving:

- Salsa
- Sour cream
- Guacamole

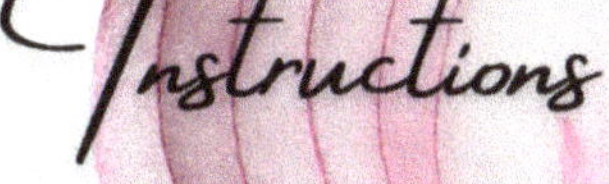 Instructions

1. In a skillet, heat a dash of olive oil. Sauté the diced bell pepper and onion until they're soft and fragrant. Add the ham and cook for a few more minutes. Pour in the beaten eggs, scrambling them with the veggies and ham. Season with salt and pepper.

2. Lay out the gluten-free tortillas. Sprinkle cheese on one half of each tortilla, then spoon the egg mixture on top. Fold the tortillas over to create a half-moon shape.

3. In the same skillet, cook the quesadillas for 2-3 minutes on each side, until the tortillas are golden and the cheese has melted. Mia and Stella can help with assembling their own quesadillas – a perfect task for little hands!

4. Cut the quesadillas into wedges and serve with salsa, sour cream, and guacamole. It's a build-your-own breakfast adventure!

And just like that, our Breakfast Quesadillas turn an ordinary morning into a celebration of flavours and fun. The kitchen echoes with the sounds of satisfaction – the crunch of the tortillas, the oohs and aahs over each cheesy bite, and the playful debates about tomorrow's potential quesadilla fillings. Stella, with a cheeky grin, suggests, "Maybe we can sneak in some chocolate chips next time?" while Mia, with a twinkle in her eye, counters, "Or how about some strawberries?" Their imaginations run wild with quesadilla possibilities.

BANANA Oat Muffins

Ah, the serene battlefield of the breakfast table, where the clash of spoons and the rally of cereal bowls reign supreme. As the self-appointed general of the morning routine, I've seen my fair share of skirmishes over anything green or, heaven forbid, fibrous. Enter the game-changer, the secret weapon in my arsenal of parental trickery: Banana Oatmeal Muffins. They're the culinary equivalent of a trojan horse, sneaking in nutrition under the guise of deliciousness.

Imagine the scene: the sun peeks over the horizon, birds chirping their morning tune, and the scent of banana oatmeal muffins wafting through the air, luring my little warriors to the table. They approach, skeptical yet intrigued, unaware of the nutritional ninja hiding within these fluffy morsels.

Ingredients

- 2 large ripe bananas
- 2 ½ cups old-fashioned oats
- 1 cup plain low-fat Greek yogurt
- 2 large eggs
- ⅓ cup honey
- 1 ½ teaspoons baking powder
- ½ teaspoon baking soda

Instructions

1. Preheat your oven to 400°F. Line your muffin pan with waxed paper or foil liners or give it a good grease to ensure your muffins don't stage a sticky rebellion.

2. Now, here's where the magic happens. In your blender (or trusty food processor), assemble the dream team: the ripe bananas, the oats, the Greek yogurt (your secret agent in creamy disguise), the eggs (your loyal sidekicks), the honey (or sugar if you're feeling sweetly daring), the baking powder (the liftoff specialist), and the baking soda (to make your muffins as light as a feather). Blend this crew until they're smoother than your negotiation skills when convincing your kids to eat veggies.

3. Divide this devious batter among your cupcake liners. They should be about ¾ full. Think of them as your little army, ready to conquer the morning hunger battlefield.

4. Now, it's time to bake. Pop them in your preheated oven and let them bake for 18-20 minutes. How do you know they're ready to face the day? Stick a toothpick in one muffin; if it comes out clean, consider your mission accomplished.

And there you have it, Banana Oatmeal Muffins – your secret weapon for breakfast battles. They're so good that your kids will be left wondering, "Did we just win the war against healthy eating?" Enjoy your victory, parent warriors!

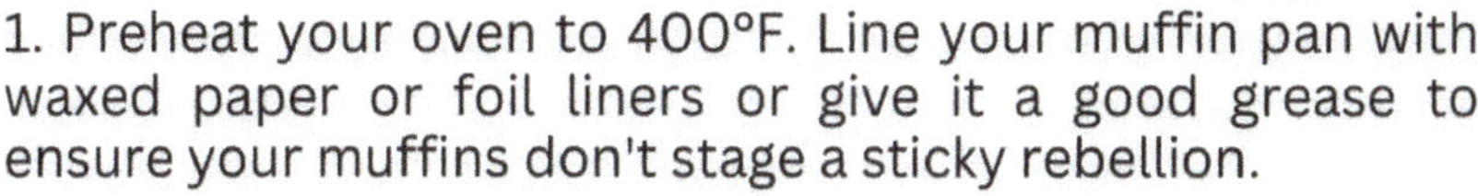

SWEET POTATO
Toast

Let's face it, parents: the breakfast routine can get a little... stale. But fear not, because I've got a game-changer for you – Sweet Potato Toast with Peanut Butter & Jelly! It's the breakfast remix your taste buds have been begging for.

Ingredients

- 2 medium sweet potatoes
- ½ cup peanut butter
- ¼ cup strawberry jelly or fresh-cut fruit
- anything you want to put on it

Instructions

1. First, gather your sweet potatoes, the unsung heroes of this breakfast revolution. Place them on a large cutting board and give them a little trim by slicing off the ends.

2. Now, for the magic touch. Slice those sweet potatoes lengthwise into ¼-inch slabs with a large knife. You should get about 4 slices per potato, but feel free to slice more if you're feeling extra hungry.

3. Time to toast, but we're not talking about your regular bread here. Place those sweet potato slices in the toaster oven and let them work their magic. Toast until they reach that perfect level of lightly browned and fork-tender in the center. If you're using a regular toaster, stand those sweet potato slices up and give them a double toasting cycle. Trust me; it's worth it!

4. Once your sweet potato slices are like golden rays of sunshine, it's time to bring in the flavor brigade. Spread that creamy peanut butter over each sweet potato slice, covering them like a warm, nutty hug.

5. And now, the sweet twist. Follow up with a generous dollop of strawberry jam, letting it ooze and mingle with the peanut butter. It's the dynamic duo your taste buds have been craving.

There you have it, Sweet Potato Toast with Peanut Butter & Jelly – a breakfast revelation that'll have your kids saying, "Can we have this every day?" Enjoy the burst of flavor, and let the breakfast remix begin!

Breakfast Cookies

Ah, fall! A time for cozy sweaters, crunchy leaves, and... covert kitchen operations? Let me set the scene: there I was, ready to whip up my famous Pumpkin Pie Breakfast Cookies. Enter my twin accomplices, with twinkles in their eyes and a secret plan up their tiny sleeves. As I turned to grab the oats, they made their move, stealthily adding a handful of chocolate chips to the mix. "For extra energy, Dad!" they chimed in unison. Little did they know, their 'sneaky' addition just made a good thing even better. So, here's to fall flavours with a mischievous chocolate twist!

Prepare Time
10 Minutes

Bake Time
15 Minutes

Serves
15 Cookies

Ingredients

- ½ cup pumpkin puree (hello, pumpkin season!)
- ½ cup natural peanut butter (or nut-free alternative if you want to put them in your kids' lunch)
- ¼ cup honey
- 1 tablespoon vanilla extract
- 1 ¼ cup quick oats
- 2 teaspoons pumpkin pie spice
- ½ teaspoon baking powder
- chocolate chips (Thanks to me and Stella) but totally optional

Instructions

1. To kickstart your pumpkin breakfast adventure, preheat your oven to 350°F. Grab a trusty cookie sheet and line it with parchment paper, making cleanup a breeze.

2. In a spacious bowl, combine the star of the show – pumpkin puree – with your choice of natural peanut butter or a nut-free alternative if allergies are in the mix. Add a generous drizzle of honey for that touch of natural sweetness, and don't forget the vanilla extract to cozy things up.

3. Now, let's create that perfect texture. Add the quick oats, a quintessential element in these breakfast cookies. Sprinkle in the pumpkin pie spice to infuse that unmistakable fall aroma, and add a dash of baking powder for that magical lift.

4. Mix everything together until your oats are thoroughly coated in that pumpkin goodness, creating a dough that screams fall flavours.

5. Using a trusty cookie scooper, drop delightful mounds of dough onto your prepared cookie sheets, making sure to leave about 2 inches of space between each. Now, using your hands, gently flatten and shape each mound into a cookie form.

6. Slide your cookie sheet into the preheated oven and let the magic happen for about 15 minutes. When they emerge, they should be golden and smelling like a pumpkin spice dream. Let them cool down, resisting the urge to devour them all at once.

And there you have it – Pumpkin Pie Breakfast Cookies, a scrumptious way to savour the flavours of fall during those busy mornings. Enjoy the warmth and comfort of pumpkin pie without the fuss!

PROTEIN-PACKED

Smoothies

Raising energetic kids can sometimes feel like a never-ending quest. You want them to have the energy they need for their adventures, but getting them to eat the right things can be a challenge. That's where our Protein-Packed Smoothies come to the rescue!

Ingredients

- 2 cups plain Greek yogurt
- 2 ripe medium bananas
- 2 cups sliced fresh strawberries or frozen unsweetened strawberries
- 2 tablespoons honey
- 2 tablespoons peanut butter
- Whole fresh strawberries (optional)

Instructions

1. In the realm of blenders, gather your Greek yogurt, ripe bananas, sliced strawberries, honey, and the trusty sidekick, peanut butter. They're about to embark on a delicious journey.

2. Toss them all into the blender and cover it, ready for action. It's blending time! Let the blender work its magic until the mixture is almost as smooth as your kid's adventures. Occasionally, pause to scrape down the sides, making sure every ingredient joins the party.

3. Now, it's time to share the bounty. Divide this liquid gold among four glasses, each one a vessel of energy and nutrition. If you're feeling fancy, top them off with whole strawberries for that extra touch of awesomeness.

These Protein-Packed Smoothies are the secret weapon to keep your little explorers fueled and ready for their next adventure. After all, superheroes need their superfood! Share your smoothie creations with me on Instagram @thedaddiaries.ca.

Apple Crumble

✓ **Prepare Time**
10 Minutes

✓ **Bake Time**
30 Minutes

✓ **Serves**
6

If you're like me, you're always on the lookout for quick and healthy treats that your family will love, and we've got just the thing: my "Guilt Free - Apple Crumble," a wholesome twist on the classic apple crumble. Get ready to indulge in the flavours of fall without any guilt.

Ingredients

- 2 lb (1kg) of fresh, crisp apples, diced
- 1 cup of maple syrup (or honey)
- 1 teaspoon of ground cinnamon
- 2 tablespoons of water
- 1 cup of rolled oats
- 1 cup of almond flour
- 1 tablespoon of sliced almonds
- 1/2 cup of melted coconut oil
- 1/2 teaspoon of salt to balance the flavours

Instructions

1. To kickstart your pumpkin breakfast adventure, preheat your oven to 350°F. Grab a trusty cookie sheet and line it with parchment paper, making cleanup a breeze.

2. In a spacious bowl, combine the star of the show – pumpkin puree – with your choice of natural peanut butter or a nut-free alternative if allergies are in the mix. Add a generous drizzle of honey for that touch of natural sweetness, and don't forget the vanilla extract to cozy things up.

3. Now, let's create that perfect texture. Add the quick oats, a quintessential element in these breakfast cookies. Sprinkle in the pumpkin pie spice to infuse that unmistakable fall aroma, and add a dash of baking powder for that magical lift.

4. Mix everything together until your oats are thoroughly coated in that pumpkin goodness, creating a dough that screams fall flavours.

5. Using a trusty cookie scooper, drop delightful mounds of dough onto your prepared cookie sheets, making sure to leave about 2 inches of space between each. Now, using your hands, gently flatten and shape each mound into a cookie form.

6. Slide your cookie sheet into the preheated oven and let the magic happen for about 15 minutes. When they emerge, they should be golden and smelling like a pumpkin spice dream. Let them cool down, resisting the urge to devour them all at once.

And there you have it – Pumpkin Pie Breakfast Cookies, a scrumptious way to savour the flavours of fall during those busy mornings. Enjoy the warmth and comfort of pumpkin pie without the fuss!

CHOCOLATE-COCONUT
Breakfast Balls

We're diving into a recipe that's not only so good but also packed with all the good stuff your little heroes need. I'm talking about Chocolate Coconut Energy Balls – a sneaky way to slip in some superfoods without your kids suspecting a thing. Perfect for an on-the-go breakfast.

Prepare Time
10 Minutes

Cool Time
30 Minutes

Serves
18 balls

Ingredients

- 1 cup of gluten-free old-fashioned oats
- 3/4 cup of almond butter
- 3/4 cup of dark chocolate chips
- 1/8 teaspoon of cinnamon
- 1/2 cup of flaxseed
- 2 tablespoons of chia seeds
- 1/4 teaspoon of almond extract
- 1/4 teaspoon of vanilla extract
- 1/3 cup of agave nectar or honey (your choice)
- 1/2 cup of shaved coconut

Instructions

1. In your trusty mixing bowl, gather the oats, almond butter, dark chocolate chips, a dash of cinnamon, flaxseed, chia seeds, and your sweetener of choice, whether it's agave nectar or honey. Don't forget to add the almond and vanilla extracts to the mix.

2. Now, give it all a good stir until everything becomes one happy, gooey family.

3. Time for a little chill-out session. Pop your mixture in the fridge for about 30 minutes. This helps it firm up, making it easier to shape.

4. Once it's nice and chilled, grab small portions of the mixture and roll them into 1-inch balls. But hold on, we're not done yet! Roll each of these energy balls in the shaved coconut until they're all snug and evenly coated.

5. Lay your superhero energy balls on a tray or plate lined with parchment paper. Keep them a bit spaced out, so they don't get too friendly and stick together.

6. Now, here's the best part – store these energy boosters in an airtight container in the fridge. This way, they stay fresh, delicious, and ready to fuel your little heroes whenever they need a pick-me-up.

These Chocolate Coconut Energy Balls aren't just tasty; they're sneaky nutritional powerhouses that your kids will love. So, go ahead, whip up a batch, and watch them conquer their day with the energy of superheroes! Enjoy this one-the-go breakfast!

Kid-Approved Bagels

Prepare Time
10 Minutes

Bake Time
25 Minutes

Serves
8 Bagels

Alright, folks, who's ready to embark on a bagel-making adventure with a little twist? We're talking about whipping up some mind-blowingly delicious gluten-free bagels perfect for your mornings; add some scrambled eggs on top with a slice of avocado, and trust me, you'll thank me later. And guess what? It only takes TWO ingredients!

Ingredients

- 2 cups of almond flour
- 1 cup of Greek yogurt
- 1 egg (optional, but it'll make 'em shine!)
- A generous sprinkle of Everything But the Bagel seasoning

Instructions

1. First, grab a bowl and toss in that almond flour and Greek yogurt. Now, time to get messy (the fun kind)! Mix 'em up real nice until you've got yourself a silky-smooth dough. It's like magic in the making.

2. Who's up for a little dough-kneading workout? Knead that glorious mixture for 3-5 minutes. Feel the bagel love!

3. Now, let's shape these little wonders. Roll your dough into a log, then slice it into 6 pieces. Transform each piece into a classic bagel shape, complete with the essential hole in the middle.

4. Want that extra bagel glaze and flavor? Brush on some egg wash if you like a bit of sheen, and then generously sprinkle your bagel babies with your seasoning of choice. We highly recommend "Everything But the Bagel" for the full bagel experience.

5. Preheat your oven to 375°F (190°C), and pop your creations in there for 20-25 minutes. Keep an eye on them – you want those bagels to turn into golden perfection.

And there you have it, folks – the ultimate, kid-approved, and oh-so-easy gluten-free bagels. Stella loves it with Nutella, while Mia enjoys it with some raspberry jam. Get ready for your kitchen to smell like a bagel shop, and let the bagel devouring commence!

SPICED
kid approved Donuts

Picture this: a quiet Saturday morning in the Tito household, the air filled with anticipation (and the smell of coffee). Today's mission? Gluten-free spiced donuts! The kids, Mia and Stella, are my eager kitchen assistants, each with a spoon in hand, ready for battle against the gluten-free challenge.

As I'm measuring out the cinnamon, ginger, and cloves, Stella, with a giggle, decides to double the cinnamon - "for extra magic," she says. Meanwhile, Mia, the ever-practical one, meticulously arranges the donut toppings, debating whether sprinkles are a breakfast food. Amidst the flour clouds and sugar showers, our kitchen transforms into a laugh-filled, donut factory. It's a messy, joyful chaos - with Stella declaring herself the 'Cinnamon Queen' and Mia, the 'Sprinkle Strategist.'

Prepare Time
45 Minutes

cool Time
1 Hour

Serves
48 Donuts

- 4 cups Gluten-Free Flour (Caputo)
- 2 teaspoons baking powder
- ½ teaspoon salt
- 2 eggs
- 1 ¼ cups granulated sugar
- 1 teaspoon gluten-free vanilla
- ⅔ cup milk
- ¼ cup butter, melted
- Vegetable oil or shortening for deep-fat frying
- Gluten-free powdered sugar (optional)
- 1 tsp. ground cinnamon
- 1/2 tsp. ground ginger,
- 1/8 tsp. ground cloves

1. In the world of mixing bowls, unite the Gluten-Free Mix, ground cinnamon, ground ginger, ground cloves, baking powder, and salt. Let them become friends, stirring them together.

2. In a larger bowl, beat eggs, sugar, and vanilla with a mixer on medium for 3 minutes, or until they're thickened and ready for the donut transformation.

3. In a smaller bowl, introduce milk and melted butter, letting them get to know each other.

4. Now, it's time for the grand assembly. Add the flour mixture and milk mixture to the egg mixture alternately, giving each addition a moment to blend in. Stir gently after each addition, ensuring they combine harmoniously. If needed, you can stir in the last bit of the flour mixture.

5. Cover this delightful donut dough and let it chill for an hour, or until it's ready to be shaped into sweet rings.

6. Sprinkle a work surface with a little more of the flour mix. Roll the dough to a thickness of 1/2 inch. Using a floured 2 1/2-inch donut cutter, cut out your donuts. Dip the cutter into the flour mix as needed between cuts and don't forget to reroll any dough scraps.

7. In a large, heavy saucepan, let 1 to 2 inches of oil heat up to a toasty 365°F. It's time for the donuts to take a dip! Fry them, two or three at a time, for about 2 minutes or until they're golden, turning them once for an even tan. Use a slotted spoon to rescue them and let them rest on paper towels.

8. While the donuts are still slightly warm, coat them with additional 2/3 cup granulated sugar and 1/2 tsp. ground cinnamon. Make sure they cool completely first.

And there you have it – your very own batch of gluten-free donuts. Treat your kids to a delightful and safe donut experience they won't forget.

Greek Yogurt Frosting

Prepare Time
25 Minutes

Bake Time
25 Minutes

Serves
12 Muffins

Who says gluten-free can't be incredibly delicious? These zucchini muffins are so good; even those without dietary restrictions will be reaching for seconds. Top them with Greek yogurt frosting for a little protein boost.

Ingredients

- Gluten-free nonstick cooking spray
- 1 cup gluten-free all-purpose flour
- ¼ cup granulated sugar
- ¼ cup packed brown sugar
- 1 teaspoon ground cinnamon
- ½ teaspoon baking powder
- ½ teaspoon salt
- ¼ teaspoon baking soda
- 2 eggs, lightly beaten
- ¼ cup fat-free milk
- 1 cup cooked quinoa
- 1 cup coarsely shredded zucchini
- ½ cup unsweetened applesauce
- ¼ cup canola oil
- 1 teaspoon vanilla

Greek Yogurt Frosting:
- 2 cups plain fat-free Greek yogurt
- 3 tablespoons powdered sugar
- 1 teaspoon vanilla
- ½ teaspoon finely shredded lemon peel

Instructions

1. Preheat your oven to 350°F. Lightly coat twelve 2 1/2-inch muffin cups with cooking spray; set them aside.

2. In a large bowl, stir together the flour, granulated sugar, brown sugar, cinnamon, baking powder, salt, and baking soda. Create a well in the center of the flour mixture; leave it to rest.

3. In a medium bowl, combine the eggs and milk. Stir in the quinoa, zucchini, applesauce, oil, and vanilla. Add this quinoa mixture all at once to the flour mixture, stirring gently to combine. Spoon the batter into the prepared muffin cups, filling each about three-fourths full.

4. Bake for approximately 25 minutes or until a wooden toothpick inserted in the centers comes out clean. Let the muffins cool in the muffin cups on a wire rack for 5 minutes, then remove them from the muffin cups. Allow them to cool completely on a wire rack. Before serving, spread Greek Yogurt Frosting over the muffins and sprinkle them with lemon peel.

Greek Yogurt Frosting:

1. In a small bowl, stir together the yogurt, powdered sugar, and vanilla.

Get ready for a gluten-free taste sensation that will leave your taste buds dancing. Whether you enjoy these zucchini muffins for breakfast or as an afternoon treat, they're bound to be a hit.

Toffee Banana Bread

Your kids will go absolutely bananas over the explosion of flavors in this Gluten-Free Toasted Coconut Toffee Banana Bread. It's impossible not to wake up happy with this for breakfast.

Prepare Time
15 Minutes

Bake Time
35 Minutes

Serves
3 Mini Loafs

Ingredients

- ½ cup coconut oil, room temperature (soft but not melted)
- ⅔ cup granulated sugar
- ½ cup coconut sugar
- 2 large eggs
- 1 teaspoon vanilla extract
- 2 cups plus 3 tablespoons high-quality gluten-free all-purpose flour
- 1½ teaspoons baking soda
- 1 teaspoon salt
- 1 teaspoon cinnamon
- ½ teaspoon xanthan gum (if your all-purpose doesn't have)
- ½ cup canned coconut milk (full fat)
- 1 cup mashed ripe bananas (2-3)
- ½ cup finely chopped pecan
- ½ cup toffee bits
- ½ cup sweetened coconut flakes
- ½ cup semi-sweet chocolate chips

Instructions

1. Preheat your oven to 350 degrees – the starting point for deliciousness.

2. In a large mixing bowl, blend coconut oil, granulated sugar, and coconut sugar for about 1 minute until it's all cozy and mixed. Don't forget to scrape down the sides for good measure.

3. Add eggs and vanilla extract, mixing until smooth. Let them all get to know each other.

4. In a smaller bowl, sift together the gluten-free flour, baking soda, salt, cinnamon, and xanthan gum (only if your flour mix lacks it).

5. Add half of the dry mix to the wet mix, blending gently. Pour in the coconut milk and mix until smooth. Now add the remaining dry mix and make sure everything is well combined.

6. Gently fold in mashed bananas, aiming for a soupy texture without any chunks.

7. Stir in ¼ cup of pecan pieces, ¼ cup of toffee bits, ¼ cup of sweetened coconut flakes, and ¼ cup of chocolate chips. Let the batter chill for 10 minutes to soak up the flavours.

8. Grease 3 mini loaf pans with cooking spray. Evenly distribute the batter among them.

9. Top each loaf with the remaining pecans, toffee bits, coconut flakes, and chocolate chips. Press them gently into the batter.

10. Bake on the middle oven rack at 350 degrees for 35-40 minutes until they're gloriously golden and spring back when touched or a toothpick comes out clean.

11. Take them out of the oven and let them cool on a rack. After 15 minutes, give them a gentle nudge to release from the pans and let them cool completely.

Your breakfast masterpiece is ready! It's a symphony of flavours – the rich and nutty pecans, the buttery toffee bits, the tropical twist of coconut, and the indulgent chocolate chips, all dancing with the sweet embrace of bananas. This is breakfast like you've never had before! Share your breakfast delight on Instagram @thedaddiaries.ca.

Banana Bread Bonanza

Gather 'round, my friends, for I have a tale to tell about the time I attempted to make banana bread with my two tiny terrors. It all began innocently enough when I spotted some sad-looking bananas and thought, "Why not whip up a batch of delicious bread?" Little did I know, it would turn into a comedy of errors in the kitchen.

I announced our baking plans, and my little ones were immediately on board, their excitement rivalling that of pirates discovering buried treasure. We suited up in our aprons and got to work.

First obstacle: mashing the bananas. Let me tell you, it's like God himself designed this task to test a parent's patience. The girls joyfully smashed away at the slimy fruit, sending sticky goo flying everywhere. "Look, Daddy! It's like squishy playdough!" Stella exclaimed as she flung banana bits across the counter. Meanwhile, Mia was determined to see just how far she could stretch a piece of banana. (Spoiler alert: very far.)

Then came the real fun – mixing everything together. Flour, sugar, eggs – each addition to the bowl was an adventure in itself. "Oops, too much flour!" Mia giggled as she created a blizzard of white powder. "We're in a real-life snow globe!" Stella chimed in happily, her mischievous eyes sparkling. Who needs precise measurements when you can have this much chaos?

And let's not forget the great egg-cracking debacle. Let's just say we discovered that eggshells add an unexpected crunch to banana bread. "It's added fiber," I reassured myself as I fished out yet another shell fragment from the batter. Ahh, the joys of cooking with kids – never a dull moment!

After much experimentation and chaotic mixing, we cautiously slid our concoction into the oven. The scent of burnt banana and a hint of scrambled eggs wafted through the house.

When the timer finally went off, we huddled around the oven with nervous excitement. Our banana bread creation was... well, it was definitely something. Asymmetrical, crumbly, and with an unexpected crunch thanks to some stray eggshells. But hey, the kids were proud of their masterpiece. "We just made the world's best banana bread!" exclaimed Mia, beaming with pride.

As we attempted to enjoy our quirky creation, every bite reminded us of the chaos and hilarity that ensued in the kitchen. And isn't that what baking with kids is all about? Not perfection, but making memories – even if they involve crunchy eggshell bits.

Mia
Stella
Mia

CHOCOLATE BANANA BREAD
Peanut Butter swirl

Get ready to elevate your breakfast game with this delectable Chocolate Banana Bread with a Peanut Butter Swirl. It's a twist on the classic that will have your taste buds dancing. Perfectly moist, rich, and irresistible, this recipe is a delightful indulgence your family will adore.

Prepare Time
15 Minutes

Bake Time
35 Minutes

Serves
6 Mini Loafs

Ingredients

- 1 stick of melted butter
- ½ cup of vegetable oil
- 1 cup of sugar
- ¾ cup of brown sugar
- 3 large eggs
- 2 teaspoons of vanilla
- 1½ cups of mashed ripe bananas (about 4-5)
- ½ cup of full-fat sour cream
- ½ cup of hot water

- 1 cup of cocoa powder
- 1 teaspoon of salt
- 2½ teaspoons of baking powder
- ¾ teaspoon of baking soda
- ¼ teaspoon of xanthan gum (only if your flour blend doesn't have it)
- 2½ cups of high-quality gluten-free all-purpose flour
- 2 cups semi-sweet chocolate chips
- ½ cup of natural stir peanut butter (optional)

Instructions

1. Preheat your oven to a cozy 350 degrees. Grease six mini or three standard nonstick loaf pans or prepare muffin tins.

2. Melt a stick of butter and add vegetable oil, granulated sugar, brown sugar, eggs, and vanilla. Whisk until it's smooth.

3. Mash those ripe bananas until they're soupy, add sour cream, and mix until it's all blended.

4. Prepare your chocolaty magic sauce: Heat water, add cocoa powder, and whisk until it's a smooth paste. Add it to your batter and whisk until it's pure chocolate delight.

5. Sift together salt, baking powder, baking soda, xanthan gum (if needed), and gluten-free flour. Add these dry wonders to your wet mixture and stir until they're well-acquainted.

6. Now, the best part: add 1¼ cups of chocolate chips and stir until they're part of the fun. Divide the batter into your pans, filling them about ¾ of the way.

7. For the peanut butter swirl, drizzle the melted peanut butter on top and give it a gentle swirl. Top it off with the remaining chocolate chips.

8. Bake them at 350 degrees. Mini loaves take 35-40 minutes, standard loaves need 55-65 minutes, and muffins require 18-22 minutes. Keep an eye on them until they're beautifully done.

9. Let them cool and enjoy! Store leftovers in an airtight container at room temperature for a few days, in the fridge for a week, or in the freezer for a few months. Warm them up, and you're in for a treat.

Indulge in the delightful blend of chocolate and banana goodness with a hint of peanut butter swirl. This Chocolate Banana Bread is sure to become a beloved breakfast treat, a satisfying snack, or a delightful dessert in your home. Share the love by making and enjoying this irresistible creation with your loved ones.

Breakfast Bread

Toast – the unsung hero of breakfast, the reliable sidekick to eggs, cheese, jam, and, let's be real, anything you can pile on it. But when I embarked on the treacherous journey of gluten-free living, I mourned the potential loss of my toasty companion. Fear not, fellow gluten-free warriors, for I present to you the Breakfast Bread – a toast-worthy creation that even the girls approve of. It's like winning the breakfast lottery without the gluten gamble.

Prepare Time
10 Minutes

Bake Time
30 Minutes

Serves
1 loaf

Ingredients

- 1 carrot, grated
- 1 zucchini (courgette), grated
- 1 cup sweet potato, grated
- 1/2 cup coconut milk
- 2 tbsp coconut oil
- 3 eggs, whisked
- 2 cups almond flour
- 1 tsp baking powder
- A pinch of cumin
- A pinch of salt
- Pumpkin seeds (to sprinkle on top, because we're fancy like that)

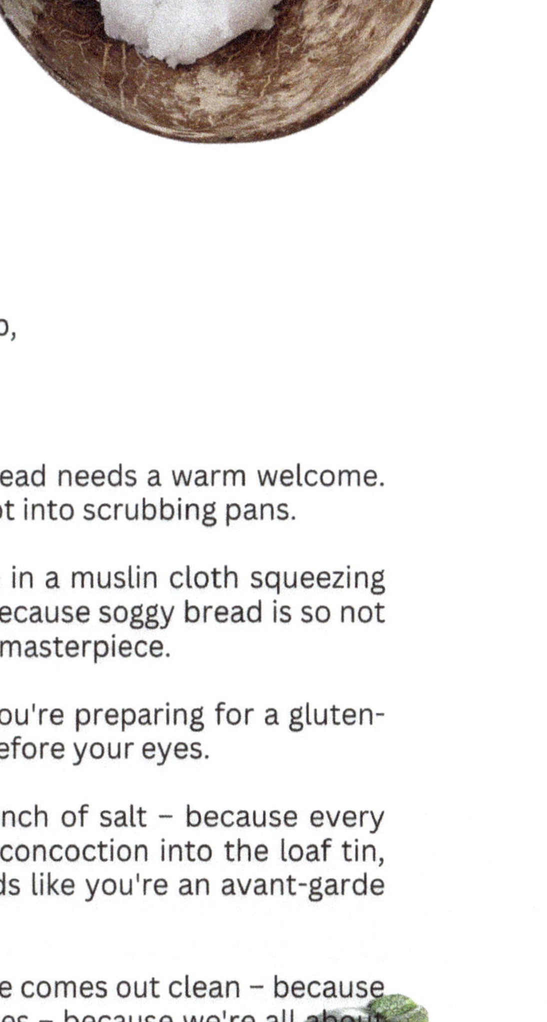

Instructions

1. Pre-heat the oven to 350°F – because even gluten-free bread needs a warm welcome. Line a loaf tin with baking paper – because we're fancy and not into scrubbing pans.

2. Grate the carrot, zucchini, and sweet potato, then engage in a muslin cloth squeezing extravaganza. Extract as much water as humanly possible – because soggy bread is so not our vibe. Dump them into a bowl like you're creating a veggie masterpiece.

3. Add the eggs, coconut milk, and coconut oil – mix it like you're preparing for a gluten-free bake-off. Marvel at the gluten-free alchemy happening before your eyes.

4. Toss in the almond flour, baking powder, cumin, and a pinch of salt – because every masterpiece needs a dash of this, a pinch of that. Pour the concoction into the loaf tin, and for the pièce de résistance, sprinkle those pumpkin seeds like you're an avant-garde chef.

5. Pop it into the oven for 30 minutes or until an inserted knife comes out clean – because gluten-free patience is a virtue. Serve it up with feta and olives – because we're all about that sophisticated brunch life.

Behold, the Gluten-Free Breakfast Bread – a toast to gluten-free mornings that won't crumble under pressure. Enjoy the gluten-free revolution, one slice at a time!

Ah, the wonders of Lemon Blueberry Bread – a gluten-free delight that's not just a breakfast champion but a lunchbox hero for the discerning taste buds of the little ones. Brace yourself for a burst of fresh flavours, fluffy texture, and the joy of a gluten-free life!

Prepare Time
30 Minutes

Bake Time
1 hour

Serves
1 large loaf + 1 mini loaf

 Ingredients

Instructions

- 2 cups all-purpose gluten-free flour containing xanthan gum
- 1 tablespoon gluten-free baking powder
- 1/2 teaspoon salt
- 3/4 cup granulated sugar or coconut sugar
- 8 tablespoons butter, melted and cooled
- 1/2 cup plain yogurt or plain almond milk yogurt
- 3 large eggs
- 1 tablespoon fresh lemon juice
- 2 packed teaspoons freshly grated lemon zest
- 1 teaspoon vanilla extract
- 1 teaspoon lemon extract, optional (add for more lemon flavour)
- 1 1/2 cups fresh blueberries, rinsed + extra rinsed blueberries for topping if desired
- 2 tablespoons Natural brown sugar

1. In a large bowl, whisk together flour, baking powder, and salt – because every good relationship starts with a solid foundation.

2. *In a separate bowl, whisk together sugar, melted butter, yogurt, eggs, lemon juice, lemon zest, vanilla extract (and lemon extract if feeling extra zesty) until the love is well combined.

3. Mix the flour mixture into the wet mixture until thoroughly combined and no lumps remain – about 1 minute of pure gluten-free symphony.

4. Gently fold in those luscious blueberries until they're evenly distributed – because each bite should be a burst of berry joy.

5. Cover the bowl with plastic wrap and let the batter rest at room temperature for 20 minutes (no longer than 30 minutes) – because good things come to those who wait.

6. Meanwhile, preheat the oven to 375 degrees and line a 10-inch loaf pan and a mini loaf pan with parchment paper OR grease and flour the pans – because a well-prepared pan is a happy pan.

7.After 20 minutes of anticipation, spoon the batter into the loaf pans and spread the joy evenly.

8. *Add extra blueberries if desired and sprinkle turbinado (raw natural brown sugar)
 sugar over the top – because presentation is everything.

9. Bake the small bread for 25 minutes, then cover loosely with foil and bake an additional 10 minutes – or until a toothpick inserted in the centre comes out clean. For the large bread, bake for 45-50 minutes, then cover loosely with foil and bake an additional 10 minutes – again, until that toothpick dance is clean.

10. *Cool & Revel:* Let the bread cool in the pans for about 30 minutes or longer, then gently remove from the pans and let it continue cooling on a wire rack – because the joy of Lemon Blueberry Bread deserves a grand entrance.

Behold, the gluten-free symphony of Lemon Blueberry Bread – where sunshine meets berries in a harmonious blend of happiness. May your mornings be brighter and your lunchboxes ever joyful! Share your Lemon Blueberry Bread on Instagram and tag me @thedaddiaries.ca.

SWEET AND FLUFFY
Cinnamon Rolls

Prepare Time
20 Minutes

Rise Time
1 Hour

Bake Time
25 Minutes

Serves
12 Rolls

Roll up your sleeves and put on your cape, because today, we're turning into gluten-free superheroes in the kitchen! Picture this: a world where the tantalizing aroma of cinnamon rolls was just a mere fantasy for the gluten-averse. Dark times, right? Well, not anymore! I'm here to lead you on an epic quest to create the fluffiest, most mouth-watering Gluten-Free Cinnamon Rolls that ever graced a baking dish. These aren't just any cinnamon rolls; they're the kind that make you pause and wonder, "Is this real life or a delicious, cinnamon-scented dream?" Spoiler alert: It's real, and it's spectacular. Let's get our baking capes on and dive into this recipe that's about to save your snack time!

Ingredients

For the Rolls:

- 3 1/4 cups all-purpose gluten-free flour blend (plus more for sprinkling)
- 1 1/2 teaspoons xanthan gum (omit if your blend already contains it)
- 1/2 cup cultured buttermilk blend powder (dry milk powder; make sure it's powder, not liquid!)
- 2 teaspoons instant yeast
- 1/4 teaspoon cream of tartar
- 1/4 teaspoon baking soda
- 2 tablespoons packed light brown sugar
- 1 teaspoon salt
- 1 teaspoon apple cider vinegar
- 2 tablespoons unsalted butter at room temperature
- 1 egg at room temperature, beaten
- 1 1/2 cups warm water

For the Filling:

- 4 tablespoons unsalted butter at room temperature
- 3/4 cup packed light brown sugar
- 1 teaspoon ground cinnamon

For the Glaze:

- 1 cup confectioners' sugar
- 1 1/4 tablespoon milk

1. Begin your cinnamon roll adventure by greasing a 9-inch x 13-inch casserole dish. Set it aside; it's going to be the stage for your sweet creation.

Making the Dough

2. In the bowl of a stand mixer fitted with the paddle attachment, combine the gluten-free flour blend, xanthan gum (if needed), buttermilk powder, yeast, cream of tartar, baking soda, and light brown sugar. Whisk these dry ingredients to ensure they're well-mixed.

3. Add the salt, and whisk once more to combine it thoroughly.

4. Now, add the apple cider vinegar, room-temperature butter, and the beaten egg. Mix everything until you have a smooth, cohesive dough.

5. With the mixer on low, gradually pour in the warm water, ensuring a slow but steady stream. The dough will gradually begin to pull away from the sides of the bowl in spots. Let it work for about 3 minutes on high speed, ensuring the dough is thoroughly mixed.

Rolling Out the Dough:

6. Turn the dough out onto a lightly floured surface. Sprinkle a little extra flour as needed to prevent sticking. Knead it gently until it becomes somewhat smoother.

7. Divide the dough in half and place one half under a tea towel to keep it from drying out. Roll out the remaining half of the dough into a 1/2-inch thick rectangle, approximately 9 inches x 12 inches.

Filling and Shaping:

8. Spread half of the softened butter evenly over the rectangle. Sprinkle half of the brown sugar on top of the butter, patting it down gently with your fingers. Sprinkle cinnamon evenly over the sugar.

9. Starting from a short side, roll the dough into a tight coil. Cut the rolls into sections, each about 2 inches wide, using dental floss, thread, or a sharp knife.

10. Place the rolls in the greased casserole dish, with about an inch of space between each. Gently press down on the top of each roll to compress the coil about one-third of the way down.

11. Repeat the same process with the other half of the dough, using the remaining butter and brown sugar.

Letting the Rolls Rise:

12. Cover the casserole dish with lightly oiled plastic wrap and place it in a warm, draft-free spot to rise. This should take about 1 hour but may take longer if the environment is cold and dry.

Baking:

13. Preheat your oven to 350°F as the dough nears the end of its rise. Once ready, remove the plastic wrap and place the dish in the center of the preheated oven.

14. Bake for approximately 25 minutes, until the cinnamon rolls turn golden brown on top and are thoroughly cooked in the middle. Remove them from the oven and allow them to cool to room temperature.

Glazing:

15. In a small bowl, combine the confectioners' sugar and milk. Mix until you have a thick paste.

16. If needed, add more milk in 1/4 teaspoon increments until the glaze is thick but pourable. Drizzle this glaze over the cooled cinnamon rolls and let it set briefly before serving.

Now, you can savour the delightful taste of gluten-free cinnamon rolls, ensuring that no one has to miss out on these beloved treats. Enjoy your sweet creation.

Mains

Strap on your aprons, everyone, because we're about to dive headfirst into the wild world of family mealtime. Trust me, it's a rollercoaster—part circus, part gourmet challenge, and a whole lot of "Are you kidding me?" moments mixed in. If you've ever found yourself juggling a toddler on your hip while sautéing veggies and somehow not burning the house down, then congratulations: You're a regular mealtime warrior.

In this chapter, we're not just making food; we're crafting sanity savers, peace keepers, and joy creators—all rolled into one steaming dish. Whether you fancy yourself the next celebrity chef or you're just trying to figure out how to not set off the smoke alarm (again), I've got something for you. This isn't just about throwing food on a plate; it's about whipping up something that'll make your taste buds sing and might just trick your kids into eating their veggies without a standoff.

So, ready your spatulas, my fellow kitchen gladiators. We're about to uncover a stash of recipes that will elevate your family dinners from frantic feedings to feasts that'll have everyone actually wanting to come to the table. And who knows? Maybe you'll even get through a meal without someone crying over spilled milk (literally or figuratively).

Baked Mac and Cheese

Buckle up, folks, because you're about to experience a cheesy apocalypse—welcome to Dad's Ultimate Baked Mac and Cheese! This isn't some half-assed, soggy cafeteria slop; this is the real deal, a full-on, no-apologies flavor bomb that'll knock your socks off and have you coming back for seconds (and thirds, who are we kidding?).

Ingredients

Prepare Time
10 Minutes

Cook Time
20 Minutes

Serves
4

- 1 box of gluten-free macaroni (I like Barilla)
- 2 eggs (whisked)
- 2 cups of evaporated milk (making this dish extra creamy)
- 2 teaspoons of powdered dry mustard (it's like the secret sauce of mac and cheese)
- 1 teaspoon of sea salt
- ½ teaspoon of black pepper
- ½ teaspoon of Tabasco (a hint of heat)
- 2 cups of shredded mild/sharp cheddar cheese
- 1 cup of shredded Parmesan cheese (for that Italian flair)
- 2 cups of shredded Velveeta cheese
- 8 tablespoons of melted butter (because butter makes everything better)

Instructions

1. Preheat your oven to a sizzling 400°F. We're about to turn up the heat on this cheesy adventure.

2. Combine the whisked eggs, evaporated milk, powdered mustard, salt, pepper, and a dash of Tabasco in a large bowl. Mix it until it's a flavour-packed concoction ready to take your taste buds on a ride.

3. Boil the gluten-free pasta according to the box's directions, but make sure it's 'al dente,' not mushy. And remember to salt the water because even pasta needs some seasoning love.

4. Drain the water and return the pasta to the pot Once the pasta is cooked to perfection. Now, pour the melted butter over the pasta and give it a good stir until every noodle is coated in buttery bliss.

5. Stir the milk and egg mixture a few times and then add it to the pasta. This is where the magic begins.

6. Add half of the cheese mix to the pot and stir over medium heat until the cheese melts into a creamy dream. Add the remaining cheeses and continue stirring until it's a cheese lover's paradise.

7. Grab a 9 x 13 baking dish and give it a quick spray with cooking spray. Then, pour your macaroni and cheese masterpiece into the dish. For that extra dose of yumminess, sprinkle some more cheddar cheese on top because there's no such thing as too much cheese.

8. Pop it into the oven for 20 to 25 minutes, and try your best to avoid devouring it all in one sitting (no promises, though).

And there you go, a dish that turns any regular old dinner into a warm, cheesy lovefest that's pretty damn delightful. This is comfort food at its absolute best, soon to be the new favorite in your household. So, dig in, all you mac and cheese fanatics! This one's going to rock your world. Enjoy!

Cheesy Cauliflower Breadsticks

Alright, brace yourselves, because we're about to make cauliflower the badass hero of the cheese world! These Cauliflower Breadsticks are so damn good, your kids won't even realize they're chomping on vegetables. Yeah, you heard that right—sneaky veggie intake wrapped in a delicious, cheesy disguise. Let's roll up our sleeves and dive headfirst into this cheesy escapade!

Prepare Time
20 Minutes

Bake Time
30 Minutes

Ingredients

- 1 medium-head cauliflower
- 1/2 cup shredded part-skim mozzarella cheese
- 1/2 cup grated Parmesan cheese
- 1/2 cup shredded cheddar cheese
- 1 large egg
- 1/4 cup chopped fresh parsley
- 1 garlic clove, minced (because garlic makes everything better)
- 1 teaspoon salt (for that perfect balance of flavours)

Instructions

1. Begin by processing the medium head of cauliflower in batches in a food processor until it's finely ground. Think of it as turning cauliflower into "cauli-snow."

2. Microwave your cauli-snow, covered, in a microwave-safe bowl on high until it becomes tender. That's about 8 minutes of cauliflower transformation time.

3. Once your cauliflower has cooled down a bit, wrap it up in a clean kitchen towel and give it a good squeeze to remove any excess moisture. We want our breadsticks to be cheesy, not soggy.

4. Now, back to the bowl it goes! In another bowl, mix together the shredded mozzarella, grated Parmesan, and shredded cheddar cheese. It's a cheesy trio that'll make your taste buds dance.

5. Stir half of this glorious cheese mixture into the cauliflower mix, saving the rest for later, like a cheese secret waiting to be revealed.

6. In yet another bowl (we're on a roll here), combine the large egg, chopped fresh parsley, minced garlic clove, and a teaspoon of salt. Mix this flavour-packed concoction into the cauliflower and cheese blend. It's like a cheesy symphony.

7. On a baking sheet lined with parchment paper, shape the cauliflower mix into an 11x9-inch rectangle. It's the canvas for your cheesy masterpiece.

8. Pop it into a preheated oven at 425°F and bake until the edges are gloriously golden brown. That'll take about 20-25 minutes, but keep an eye on it.

9. And now, the grand finale: top your cauliflower creation with the reserved cheese mixture and bake again until it's melted and bubbling with cheesy goodness. That's about 10-12 minutes of cheesy anticipation.

10. Finally, cut your masterpiece into 12 breadsticks, and if you're feeling fancy, serve them up with some marinara sauce for dipping. Because every superhero deserves a sidekick.

There you have it, your homemade Cauliflower Breadsticks—a cheesy sensation that'll have your family asking for more. Enjoy this delightful veggie twist on a classic favorite!

DAD'S ULTIMATE
Fried Rice

Alright, everyone, buckle up because we're diving into the world of Fried Rice—a dish so packed with flavors it'll knock your taste buds into next week. This isn't just your average, everyday side dish; it's a full-on flavor explosion that's sure to impress even the pickiest eaters around your table. So grab your apron—it's time to get cooking and show that rice who's boss!

Prepare Time
10 Minutes

Cook Time
10 Minutes

Serves
4

Ingredients

- 1 tablespoon Sesame Oil
- 1 tablespoon Oil
- 1 teaspoon Minced Garlic
- 1 teaspoon Ground Ginger (or fresh grated ginger, or the crushed ginger in the tube)
- ¼ teaspoon Crushed Red Pepper Flakes
- ¼ cup Chopped Green Onions (just the white part, save the green part for garnish)
- ½ pound Ground Turkey
- 1 cup Chopped Carrots (
- 2 cups Cooked Rice
- 3 tablespoons Gluten-Free Soy Sauce
- 2 Eggs, beaten
- 1 cup Frozen Peas

Instructions

1. Start by heating up your pan over medium/high heat. You'll know it's ready when a drop of water does a little dance on the surface, sizzling away in a flash.

2. To this sizzling canvas, add the sesame oil, regular oil, minced garlic, ginger, and a dash of crushed red pepper flakes. Let the aromas dance in the air, infusing the kitchen with a symphony of flavours.

3. Toss in the white part of the green onions, letting them join the fragrant fiesta. Keep cooking until the garlic takes on a golden hue, signalling its readiness to dazzle your taste buds.

4. Time to introduce the ground turkey to the party! Stir it up, breaking it into flavorful bits, and let it cook until it's beautifully browned.

5. Now, it's the carrots' turn to shine. Add them to the mix and let them cook for 2-3 minutes, just until they're crisp-tender, offering that delightful crunch.

6. Toss in cooked rice and gluten-free soy sauce. In about 3-4 minutes, your rice will be golden brown and heated through, ready to steal the spotlight.

7. Create a cozy "well" in the centre of your skillet – Pour in those beaten eggs and let them scramble, gradually pulling in the surrounding rice, meat, and veggies.

8. Once the egg is perfectly integrated, turn off the heat and sprinkle in those frozen peas. They'll add a burst of colour and a touch of sweetness to the ensemble.

9. Last but not least, garnish with the green part of the green onions – a final flourish that adds both colour and freshness to your culinary masterpiece.

And there you have it, fellow kitchen maestros! Dad's Flavour-Packed Fried Rice is not just a recipe; it's a culinary adventure that's bound to make you the reigning chef in your household. So, plate up and savour the delicious triumph you've just created. Bon appétit!

SHRIMP COCONUT
Fried Rice

Alright, let's crank up the heat and throw together some Shrimp Coconut Fried Rice that'll transport your kitchen straight to the tropics. This dish isn't just exploding with bold flavors—it's also got that perfect crunch and freshness that'll make your taste buds think they're on vacation. Trust me, you're about to impress the hell out of everyone, maybe even yourself.

Prepare Time
15 Minutes

Cook Time
18 Minutes

Serves
4

Instructions

1. Let's start by cooking the rice. Follow the instructions on the package; it usually takes about 8-10 minutes. Once it's cooked, set it aside.

2. While the rice is doing its thing, let's work on the other magical ingredients. In a small bowl, whisk together the soy sauce, ginger powder, and black pepper. Set this flavour-packed mixture aside.

3. Now, get a large skillet or wok ready. Heat up both the coconut oil and vegetable or peanut oil over medium heat. Once they're sizzling, add those plump shrimp. Cook them, stirring occasionally, for about 3-4 minutes or until they turn that beautiful shade of pink. Don't forget to season them with a pinch of salt and pepper. Once they're done, scoop them out onto a plate or in a bowl using a slotted spoon.

4. It's time to introduce the onion and bell pepper to the party. Toss them into the skillet, and let them cook over medium-low to medium heat. Keep stirring, and in about 3 minutes, those veggies should have softened up nicely. Now, stir in the coconut flakes, and then add the glorious mango cubes. Cook it all together, stirring constantly, for about 2 more minutes.

5. Bring back the reserved soy sauce mixture and let it heat up for about 1 minute. Then, add the rice to the mix. Keep stirring like a champ, and in about 2 minutes, your rice should be heated through. Don't forget to invite the cooked shrimp back to the skillet and adjust the seasoning with salt and pepper. Finally, sprinkle in the cilantro or parsley to add a burst of fresh flavor.

6. Serve your Shrimp Coconut Fried Rice immediately, and let your taste buds embark on a tropical adventure right in your own kitchen.

And there you go, folks—a dish so good it's like sticking your taste buds on a plane to paradise. Enjoy this little escape on a plate, and congrats on nailing another kitchen adventure. Keep on cooking, champs!

Ingredients

- 2 cups of White Rice
- 2 tablespoons of GF soy sauce
- 1 teaspoon of ginger powder
- ½ teaspoon of ground black pepper
- 2 tablespoons of coconut oil
- 1 tablespoon of vegetable or peanut oil
- 1 pound of jumbo shrimp (peeled, deveined, tail off)
- Salt and freshly ground black pepper to taste
- 1 red onion, diced
- 1 red bell pepper, de-seeded and diced
- 2-3 tablespoons of unsweetened coconut flakes
- 1 cup of frozen mango cubes
- ⅓ cup of chopped cilantro or parsley

It was a typical Tuesday evening in the Monteleone-Tito household, but what was about to unfold was anything but ordinary. On the menu was something we hadn't planned – a spontaneous stir-fry, concocted from an array of colorful veggies and whatever else we could find in the fridge. The catch? We were turning it into a game, a culinary challenge where Mia and Stella were the judges.

As Frank and I donned our aprons, the girls were already rummaging through the vegetable drawer, declaring their finds with excitement. "Look, Dad, purple carrots!" Mia exclaimed, holding them up like a prized trophy. Stella, meanwhile, unearthed a zucchini and waved it like a magic wand.

The game was simple: Frank and I would each create a stir-fry, and the girls would decide which one was the most delicious (or at least the most creative). The kitchen counter turned into our battleground, strewn with bell peppers, snap peas, mushrooms, and an assortment of sauces and spices.

Frank, always the comedian, pretended to be a famous chef on a cooking show, narrating his every move with exaggerated flair. "And now, the secret ingredient," he announced, adding a splash of soy sauce with a magician's gesture. I countered with my own theatrical technique, flipping vegetables in the pan with a flourish, eliciting giggles from our audience.
Mia and Stella hopped around, offering suggestions and occasionally sneaking bites of veggies. "More garlic!" Stella advised, while Mia insisted on adding pineapple for a sweet twist. Our kitchen was a symphony of sizzling pans, laughter, and the occasional playful dispute over who the better chef was.

Finally, the moment of truth arrived. We presented our dishes, each a vibrant mosaic of vegetables and chicken. Mia and Stella took their judging roles seriously, tasting each dish with thoughtful expressions. "I like Daddy's because it's sweeter," Mia declared after careful consideration. "But Papa's has more colors!" Stella added, diplomatically.

In the end, the verdict was a tie – both stir-fries declared winners for their unique flavors and the fun we had making them. As we sat down to eat, our plates a mix of both creations, the kitchen filled with stories, shared laughter, and plans for our next culinary adventure.

That evening, our spontaneous stir-fry spectacular was more than just a meal; it was a celebration of our family – our quirks, creativity, and the joy we find in the simplest moments together. It was a reminder that the best recipes aren't always found in cookbooks, but in the laughter and love shared around the kitchen.

Spontaneous Stir-Fry

Prepare Time
20 Minutes

Cook Time
10 Minutes

Serves
4

CHICKEN AND VEGGIE
Stir-Fry

Picture this: It's a typical Tuesday evening. The clock's ticking towards dinner time, and my kitchen is buzzing with the energy of my two little sous-chefs, Mia and Stella. They're on a mission to "inspect" every vegetable. Mia holds up a broccoli floret, inspecting it like a rare gem, while Stella pokes suspiciously at a carrot slice, her nose scrunched up in doubt.

As I start chopping the chicken, I announce, "Tonight, we're making veggies disappear!" Mia's eyes widen with intrigue, while Stella's skepticism remains. "Into our tummies!" I add with a flourish, sparking giggles from my mini culinary critics.

Into the pan goes the chicken, sizzling as it hits the heat, followed by the colourful array of veggies. The girls watch in awe as I flip and stir, transforming the ingredients into a mouth-watering spectacle. "Now, for the magic seasoning!" I declare, adding a dash of this and a sprinkle of that.

The real magic, though? Watching those once-suspect veggies vanish off their plates, faster than a magician's rabbit! "Papa, can we make veggies disappear again tomorrow?" Mia asks, already planning our next kitchen escapade.

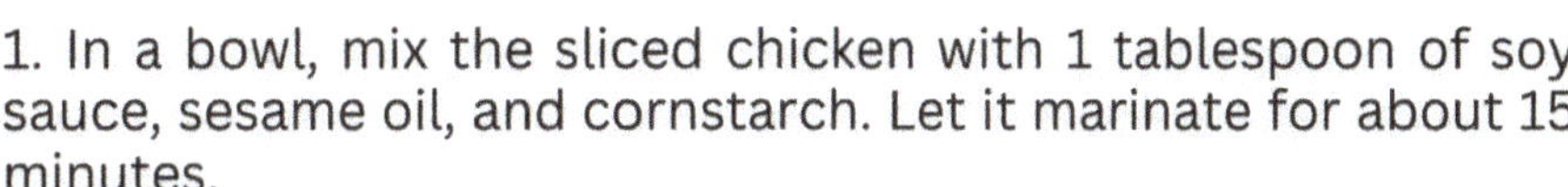

Ingredients

- 2 large chicken breasts, thinly sliced
- 3 tablespoons gluten-free soy sauce (or tamari)
- 1 tablespoon sesame oil
- 1 tablespoon cornstarch (or tapioca flour for a healthier option)
- 2 tablespoons olive oil
- 1 red bell pepper, sliced
- 1 yellow bell pepper, sliced
- 1 cup broccoli florets
- 1 medium carrot, thinly sliced
- 2 cloves garlic, minced
- 1 teaspoon fresh ginger, grated
- Salt and pepper, to taste
- Optional: 1 teaspoon chili flakes for a bit of heat
- Cooked rice or quinoa, to serve

Instructions

1. In a bowl, mix the sliced chicken with 1 tablespoon of soy sauce, sesame oil, and cornstarch. Let it marinate for about 15 minutes.

2. Heat 1 tablespoon of olive oil in a large skillet or wok over medium-high heat. Add the chicken and cook until it's browned and cooked through. Remove the chicken and set aside.

3. In the same skillet, add another tablespoon of olive oil. Toss in the bell peppers, broccoli, and carrot. Stir-fry for about 4-5 minutes until they're vibrant and slightly tender. Add the garlic and ginger, and cook for another minute.

4. Return the chicken to the skillet with the vegetables. Add the remaining soy sauce (and chili flakes if using). Stir everything together and cook for another 2-3 minutes. Season with salt and pepper to taste.

5. Serve your delicious stir-fry over a bed of rice or quinoa for a complete meal.

And that, my friends, is how you turn a simple stir-fry into an evening of laughter, culinary magic, and clean plates. Bon appétit from the Tito family's table to yours!

Hey there, kitchen adventurers! Get ready for a nugget adventure that's so easy, delicious, and, most importantly, a hit with the whole family. We're talking about Dad's Crunchy Chicken Nuggets. Seriously, they're so easy to make, they practically cook themselves!

Prepare Time
5 Minutes

Air Fry
10 Minutes

Ingredients

- 300g shredded chicken (the star of the show)
- 1 large egg (the binder)
- 1 cup of cheddar (for that cheesy goodness)
- Your favourite spicy seasonings (to add a kick)

Instructions

1. Make sure the chicken is cooked and shredded. Give it a gentle squeeze with a paper towel to remove excess moisture. We want these nuggets to be crispy, not soggy.

2. In a mixing bowl, combine the drained chicken, a whisked large egg (our trusty binder), a generous cup of cheddar cheese (because, let's be real, everything's better with cheese), and your favourite spicy seasonings. This is where you get to add your personal touch. Whether it's a pinch of cayenne, a dash of paprika, or a sprinkle of chili powder, make it as mild or wild as your taste buds desire.

3. Now comes the fun part! Shape your chicken mixture into nugget-sized delights. These can be traditional nugget shapes, mini patties, or whatever your culinary imagination dreams up.

4. Fire up your air fryer to 400°F (200°C). It's the magic appliance that'll give us crispy nuggets without all the frying fuss. Pop them into the air fryer for about 10 minutes. You'll know they're ready when they turn golden brown and irresistibly crunchy.

5. Don't have an air fryer? No problem! Preheat your oven to 400°F (200°C). Place your nuggets on a baking sheet lined with parchment paper, and slide them into the oven for approximately 20 minutes. Keep an eye on them, and when they reach that golden perfection, they're good to go.

6. Optional: You can toss your crispy nuggets in some Buffalo sauce for that extra zing. You can use your favourite dipping sauce too—plum, ranch, honey mustard, or even barbecue. The choice is yours.

So, there you have it, folks—Dad's Crunchy Chicken Nuggets. A simple, family-friendly recipe that's perfect for those busy days when you need a tasty meal on the table in no time. Enjoy the crispy, cheesy, spicy goodness, and savour every bite of this nugget adventure! They're a testament to the fact that gluten-free can be fun and delicious!

CHEESY
Big Mac bites

Let's cook up a fun snack that'll bring a smile to your families faces – Big Mac Bites. These little delights are like bite-sized burgers without the buns. Perfect for a quick snack, a school lunch or a fun meal with the family. Let's dive into the delicious details:

Ingredients

- Shredded cheddar cheese
- Hamburger meat
- Pickles
- Onions

Big Mac Sauce

- 3/4 cup mayonnaise
- 1 tbsp mustard
- 2 tbsp chopped dill pickles
- 1 tbsp white vinegar
- 1 tbsp chopped onions
- 1/2 tsp paprika
- 2 tsp sugar (optional)

Instructions

1. Cook your minced meat until brown, and add some salt and pepper to taste.

2. To kick things off, grease a muffin tin. I suggest investing in a silicone muffin tray; this makes it super easy to pop anything out of them.

3. Sprinkle a generous amount of shredded cheddar cheese into each muffin cup. You can think of it as the edible canvas for our masterpiece.

4. Here comes the star of the show – the seasoned hamburger meat. Layer it on top of that lovely cheese.

5. Grab some pickles and onions, slice them up, and place them on top of the seasoned hamburger meat.

6. And because you can never have too much cheese, let's be a little extra! Sprinkle another generous layer of shredded cheddar cheese on top of your pickle and onion toppings.

7. Now, let's get that oven fired up to 400°F (200°C). Once it's all warmed up and ready to roll, slide your loaded muffin tin inside. Let your Big Mac Bites bake in there for about 20 minutes.

8. While that's baking, in a blender, add all the ingredients for your Big Mac sauce. Blend together to make it nice and creamy.

9. Once they're done baking, take them out and let them cool for a bit. This cool-down period helps everything firm up so your bites hold together beautifully.

10. Now comes the best part – it's time to savour your cheesy Big Mac Bites! Dip them in that sauce, and you can thank me later!

There you have it; they're perfect for a quick snack, a school lunch or a fun meal with the family. Happy cooking, my fellow kitchen explorers!

BIG MAC *Tacos*

Who needs a drive-thru when you can bring the Big Mac home? Skip the car seats and create these gluten-free delights that are guaranteed to win over your toughest little food critics. Here's how to whip up Big Mac Tacos that might just become a more frequent request than bedtime stories.

Prepare Time
10 Minutes

Cook Time
10 Minutes

Ingredients

- 1 pound ground beef
- 10 gluten-free tortillas
- Cheddar cheese slices
- Shredded lettuce
- Chopped onion

Big Mac Sauce

- 3/4 cup mayonnaise
- 1 tbsp mustard
- 2 tbsp chopped dill pickles
- 1 tbsp white vinegar
- 1 tbsp chopped onions
- 1/2 tsp paprika
- 2 tsp sugar (optional)

Instructions

1. Squash a small ball of ground beef on each tortilla—think mini-burger patty meets UFO. Place beef-side down in a hot skillet. Cook for 4-5 minutes or until you can flip without causing a taco catastrophe.

2. Flip those bad boys and add a slice of cheddar directly onto the beef. Cover the pan (if you can find the lid under the pile of everything else) and let the cheese melt into ooey-gooey perfection.

3. While the meat sizzles, whisk together all the sauce ingredients in a bowl. This is your magic elixir, the key to making veggie-loaded tacos disappear.

4. Scoop in some lettuce, sprinkle those optional onions if you dare, and generously drizzle with sauce. Who knew fast food at home could be this fun and fuss-free?

Serve up these Big Mac Tacos and watch dinner disappear faster than your sanity on a long day.Here's to making mealtime a little less about the mess and a lot more about the fun!

CHEESY
Carrot Crunchies

If you're anything like me, getting your kids to eat their veggies can feel like trying to convince them that broccoli is actually a new kind of ice cream. It's an uphill battle, and sometimes, it feels impossible. But fear not, fellow parents and veggie enthusiasts, because I've got a kitchen hack that's about to change the veggie game at your dinner table.

Imagine this: your kids eagerly reaching for carrot sticks, savouring every bite with smiles on their faces. It may sound too good to be true, but these carrot sticks have that magical effect. And the best part? They're incredibly easy to make. Get ready to enjoy a veggie-packed adventure that even the pickiest eaters will adore.

Ingredients

- 1 lb carrots, medium or large-sized
- 2 tbsp olive oil for that golden crispiness
- 4 cloves garlic, minced because we're not afraid of flavour
- 1/4 cup grated parmesan cheese, the cheesy goodness
- 1/2 heaping tsp each paprika, chilli powder, onion powder and Italian herb seasoning, for that spicy kick and herbal charm
- Salt to taste, because we're all about balance
- 3/4 cup freshly grated parmesan, because cheese makes everything better

Instructions

1. Preheat your oven to a toasty 425°F. And remember, no parchment paper for this adventure!

2. Now, slice those carrots into 3-inch long pieces. And just to make things interesting, slice them in half lengthwise, so they've got a flat side to show off.

3. In a large bowl, let the olive oil, garlic, 1/4 cup grated parmesan, spices, and a pinch of salt come together in a flavour party. Toss and coat those carrot pieces in this delightful mixture.

4. Here's where the magic happens: dip the flat cut side of each carrot into the freshly grated parmesan. It's like giving them a cheesy coat of armor. Then, place them, spaced out, onto the baking sheet, cheese side down.

5. Roast your cheesy carrot comrades for 20-25 minutes or until they're golden, crispy, and ready to steal the show.

And there you have it—Crispy Parmesan Carrot Sticks that will make even the veggie skeptics in the family ask for seconds. Enjoy!

CRISPY
Parmesan Broccoli

Prepare Time
5 Minutes

Bake Time
40 Minutes

Alright, team! Today we're tackling a dish that'll make you forget all about those greasy potato chips. We're making Crispy Parmesan Broccoli! Yes, you heard right. We're turning the dreaded green trees into something the kids will fight over. Let's get to it!

Ingredients

- 3 crowns of broccoli, cut into big florets (because size matters in the veggie world)
- 10 oz of shredded parmesan cheese (that's a lot of cheesy goodness)
- Salt, garlic powder, and onion powder to taste (because flavour is our friend)

For the Spicy Ranch Dip:

- 1/2 cup mayo (the base of any good dip)
- 1/4 cup buttermilk (for that tangy kick)
- 1 tbsp Sriracha sauce (or more if you're brave)
- 1 tbsp rice vinegar (because we're fancy like that)
- 2 tbsp chopped chives (for a bit of colour)
- 1/2 tsp each onion powder and garlic powder (double trouble)
- A pinch of cayenne pepper (optional but highly recommended)

Instructions

1. Preheat your oven to 420°F. That's right, not 350, not 400, but 420. Line a baking sheet with parchment paper to avoid a cleaning nightmare later.

2. Boil water in a large pot and toss in the broccoli florets with a pinch of salt. We're just giving them a quick spa treatment, not cooking them to death, so keep it brief – a minute or two should do.

3. Spread your shredded parmesan on the baking sheet like you're laying down a cheesy carpet. Then, place your blanched broccoli on top, giving them some personal space – they're not in a crowded elevator, after all.

4. Grab a shot glass (yes, you read that right) and gently press down on each broccoli floret. It's like playing whack-a-mole but with vegetables.

5. Sprinkle with salt, garlic powder, and onion powder, then bake for 25-30 minutes. You're aiming for a golden-brown cheesy crust that'll make you forget you're eating something healthy.

6. While the broccoli bakes, mix all the dip ingredients together. Taste and adjust because you're the chef, and you make the rules.

7. Once your broccoli is crispy and golden, break it apart and watch as your family devours it faster than you can say "eat your veggies."

There you have it – a dish that's sure to turn broccoli skeptics into devout followers. Now sit back, enjoy the crunch, and take all the credit for making vegetables the star of the show!

CRISPY Cauliflower Tots

Prepare Time
5 Minutes

Bake Time
20 Minutes

If you're on a mission to sneak some extra veggies into your little one's diet or just craving a deliciously healthy snack, these Cauli Tots are about to become your new best friend. Packed with cauliflower goodness and cheesy perfection, they're so irresistible you might end up fighting your kids for the last one!

Ingredients

- 1 cup cauliflower rice, cooked & squeezed until ALL of the moisture is gone
- 1/2 cup shredded cheddar cheese
- 1 egg
- Salt & pepper

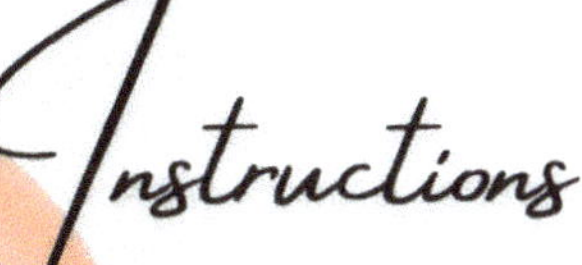

Instructions

1. Let's get started by preheating that oven to a toasty 400°F (200°C).

2. Take your cooked cauliflower rice (make sure it's dry as a desert) and toss it into a mixing bowl. Sprinkle in that lovely shredded cheddar cheese, crack in the egg, and don't forget a pinch of salt and a dash of pepper. Now, let the mixing magic happen – blend it all together until it's like a cozy cauli-cheese blanket.

3. Lay down a piece of parchment paper on a baking sheet – this will keep things mess-free. Now, scoop out spoonfuls of your cauli-cheese mixture and mold them into adorable tot shapes. You can make them as big or as bite-sized as you fancy.

4. Place your soon-to-be tots onto the baking sheet, making sure they have a little space to breathe. Pop 'em in the preheated oven and let them bake away for 20-25 minutes, or until they've transformed into crispy, golden wonders.

5. Once they're out of the oven, let them cool down just a smidge. Then, grab your favourite dipping sauce and let the dipping commence!

Enjoy these Cauli Tots as a snack, a side dish, or even as a fun appetizer for your next family gathering. They're not just a hit with the kids; they're a hit with anyone lucky enough to taste their crispy, cheesy charm. So, dig in, and let the cauliflower lovefest begin!

A SLICE OF ITALIAN TRADITION

Focaccia

Ah, the sweet scent of fresh-baked focaccia! It's like your Italian nonna's loving embrace—only gluten-free, so nobody gets a stomachache afterward. But let's be real, mastering that perfect fluff on the inside and the crunch on the outside is basically like trying to nail a Cirque du Soleil audition... in your kitchen. So, dust off your apron, because we're about to get all up in gluten-free focaccia's business, Italian-style!

Prepare Time
5 Minutes

Bake Time
25 Minutes

Rise Time
2 hours

For the Dough:
- 3 1/4 cups (455 g) Caputo gluten-free flour
- 1 tbsp plus 1 tsp (29 g) granulated sugar
- 2 tsp kosher salt
- 2 tsp rapid-rise (instant) yeast
- 2 1/2 cups (600 ml) milk
- 4 tbsp olive oil

Ingredients

For the Topping:
- About 1/4 cup extra virgin olive oil
- 2 tbsp chopped fresh rosemary
- 1 tsp sea salt
- Cracked black pepper to taste

Instructions

1. mix the gluten-free flour, sugar, salt, and yeast like a pro in a large bowl.

2. Let's get that stand mixer going with the beater blade. Start on low and pour in the milk and olive oil. Then, crank up the speed to medium for about 5 minutes.

3. Cover that bowl with plastic wrap and find a cozy, draft-free spot for it to rise. You want it to double in size, which usually takes around 2 hours.

4. Pour a generous 2-3 tablespoons of olive oil into a 12-inch cast iron skillet.

5. Plop your risen dough onto the olive oil pool, then drizzle another 2-3 tablespoons of oil on top. Use your fingers to dimple the dough and gently coax it to the edges of the skillet.

6. Cover it up and let that dough rise for about 30 minutes. It won't double in size, but it's going to stretch out a bit.

7. Heat your oven to 400 degrees. When your dough is ready, sprinkle on the rosemary, sea salt, and cracked pepper to taste.

8. Pop it in the oven for about 25-30 minutes.

9. This gluten-free focaccia is like an Italian superstar, ready to share the stage with your pasta or star in a sandwich. Slice it horizontally, and let the delicious adventures begin!

Alright, let's talk about this gluten-free focaccia. Thanks to Caputo's magic flour and a bunch of delicious toppings, this bread has become a freaking rock star in my kitchen. Seriously, it's like a little slice of Italian heaven, but without the gluten—because who needs that drama? It's so good, it might just make you believe in miracles.

RAINBOW *Pizza*

Prepare Time
45 Minutes

Bake Time
15 Minutes

Serves
12' Pizza

Today's mission: Rainbow Pizza! It's a dish as fun to make as it is to eat, and it's guaranteed to turn your kitchen into a laughter-filled art studio. Let's unleash the power of veggies in a way that even the most veggie-skeptical kiddo (yes, looking at, Mia and Stella!) can't resist.

For the Dough:
- 2 cups gluten-free all-purpose flour
- 1 t-shop Xanthan Gum (if your flour doesn't have)
- 1 packet instant yeast
- 1 teaspoon sugar
- 1 teaspoon salt
- 1 tablespoon olive oil
- ¾ cup warm water

Ingredients

For the Topping:
- ½ cup tomato sauce
- 2 cups shredded mozzarella cheese (or dairy-free alternative)
- Red cherry tomatoes, halved
- Orange bell pepper, thinly sliced
- Yellow corn
- Green broccoli florets, blanched
- Purple onions, chopped
- A handful of black olives, sliced

Instructions

1. In a large bowl, whisk together gluten-free flour, yeast, sugar, and salt. Add olive oil and warm water. Mix until a dough forms. Knead on a floured surface for a few minutes, then let it rest for about 30 minutes.

2. Get your oven nice and hot at 425°F (220°C). Meanwhile, gather the troops for veggie-chopping fun. Let's make it a game - who can slice the most colourful bell pepper?

3. Once the dough has rested, roll it out on a floured surface. Aim for a circle or, for extra fun, go for a funky shape!

4. Spread tomato sauce over the base and sprinkle with a generous layer of cheese. Here's where the magic happens!

5. Now, it's art time with food! Arrange the veggies in concentric circles by color - purple onions, orange peppers, green broccoli, yellow corn, orange peppers, red tomatoes, yellow corn, and so on. Each veggie is a paint stroke on our edible canvas.

6. Slide the pizza into the oven for 12-15 minutes or until the crust is crispy and the cheese is bubbly and golden.

7. Let the pizza cool for a bit (hardest part, I know!) and then slice it up. Watch as the colours pop and the flavours blend in a delightful dance.

And there you have it - a Gluten-Free Rainbow Pizza that's a feast for the eyes and the belly. It's not just dinner; it's a culinary adventure that turns picky eaters into veggie lovers and kitchen time into family fun time. Enjoy the laughter, the mess, and, of course, the deliciousness!

GLUTEN-FREE Pesto

This gluten-free pesto recipe is your golden ticket to flavour town! Whizz it up in bulk at home, and you've got weeks of pasta, salad, and everything nice ahead. It's a breeze to make, thanks to the trusty food processor. Here's the lowdown:

Prepare Time
5 Minutes

Ingredients

- 60g fresh basil leaves
- 40g toasted pine nuts
- Good pinch of salt
- 35g grated parmigiano reggiano
- 150ml extra virgin olive oil
- 2 garlic cloves

Instructions

1. Throw all these flavour heroes into your food processor and let the blitzing begin! Pulse until you achieve the smoothest symphony of flavours. Don't forget to scrape down the sides, so there are no unwanted lumps or giant basil surprises.

2. If you're planning for the future (up to 2 weeks, to be precise), pour your pesto into a tub and give it a cozy blanket of extra olive oil. This little trick keeps the pesto looking as vibrant as your taste buds feel. Store it in the fridge, and every time you dip into this green goodness, make sure to crown it with a fresh layer of oil before tucking it back in. You can also put it in ice trays and freeze it.

In our house, we adore pesto, and this recipe? It's like a time machine to that first magical bite in Genova. Because sometimes, the simplest things bring the most joy. Get ready to elevate your meals with a dollop, scoop, or generous pour of this homemade pesto perfection!

SPAGHETTI
al Pesto

If you're like me, you've probably had your fair share of gluten-free pasta mishaps that left you wondering if you'd ever enjoy a plate of spaghetti without the gluten-free blues. Well, fear not! Today, we're diving headfirst into a culinary journey that's so delicious that even gluten might get a little jealous. We're talking about gluten-free spaghetti, the unsung hero of pasta, paired with a pesto so green it could make the Hulk envious. So, grab your apron and your sense of humour because we're about to whip up a plate of pasta that'll have you saying, 'Gluten who?' Let's get cooking.

Ingredients

- 12 ounces (340g) gluten-free spaghetti
- 2 cups fresh basil leaves
- 1/2 cup grated Parmesan cheese
- 1/2 cup pine nuts, toasted
- 2 cloves garlic, minced
- 1/2 cup extra-virgin olive oil
- Salt and pepper to taste
- Grated Parmesan cheese for garnish (optional)

Instructions

1. Cook the gluten-free spaghetti according to the package instructions until al dente. Drain and set aside.

2. In a food processor, combine the fresh basil, grated Parmesan cheese, toasted pine nuts, and minced garlic. Pulse until the ingredients are finely chopped.

3. While the food processor is running, slowly drizzle in the extra-virgin olive oil until the mixture forms a smooth pesto. If needed, you can add more olive oil to achieve your desired consistency.

4. Season the pesto with salt and pepper to taste. Adjust the seasoning if necessary.

5. In a large mixing bowl, toss the cooked gluten-free spaghetti with the pesto sauce until well coated.

6. If desired, add the halved cherry tomatoes to the pasta and gently mix them in.

7. Serve the gluten-free spaghetti and pesto with a sprinkle of grated Parmesan cheese on top, if you like.

8. Enjoy your delicious gluten-free pasta with homemade pest

Enjoy this simple yet flavor-packed Spaghetti Aglio e Olio – a dish that not only fills your belly but also carries the warmth of tradition and fond memories. Buon Appetito!

SPAGHETTI
Aglio e olio

Ah, Spaghetti Aglio e Olio – the simplicity of its preparation, the richness of its flavors, and the memories it holds. This delightful dish was a star at wedding, an Italian tradition where it gets served at midnight, a cherished Italian staple from my upbringing. Let me share this super easy recipe with you:

Ingredients

- A box of gluten-free spaghetti
- 2 heads of garlic
- ½ cup olive oil
- 2 tablespoons butter
- ⅓ teaspoon salt (adjust to taste)
- ½ teaspoon red pepper flakes (optional; add more for extra spice)
- optional garnishes: chopped fresh parsley, freshly-grated Parmesan cheese

Instructions

1. Boil the gluten-free spaghetti following the package instructions until it reaches that perfect al dente texture.

2. While the pasta is doing its thing, peel the garlic cloves and thinly slice each one. Who cares about precision!

3. In a large skillet, combine the sliced garlic with the olive oil. Cook over medium-low heat until the garlic turns a beautiful golden brown. Be watchful – we want golden, not burnt!

4. Once the garlic hits that golden perfection, rescue it from the heat by adding about ¼ cup of the boiling pasta water. This not only stops the cooking but also infuses the garlic essence into the water.

5. Introduce the salt, butter, and red pepper flakes to the garlicky symphony. Give it a good stir.

6. As soon as your pasta achieves al dente excellence, drain it and add it to the skillet. Now, here's where the magic happens. Use your trusty tongs to toss the spaghetti, ensuring every strand is enveloped in the glorious garlic mixture.

Enjoy this simple yet flavor-packed Spaghetti Aglio e Olio – a dish that not only fills your belly but also carries the warmth of tradition and fond memories. Buon Appetito!

Prepare Time
30 Minutes

Cook Time
10 Minutes

Instructions

All right, my fellow kitchen adventurers, gear up for a gnocchi-making journey that's as exciting as it is delicious! We're diving into the world of Vegan Pumpkin Gnocchi, and trust me, this recipe is a kid-approved masterpiece.

1. Take a pot filled with salted water and bring it to a boil. This is like the stage where you're revving up your engines before a big race.

2. Peel the skin off the potatoes. Once the water is at a rolling boil, toss those peeled potatoes in and let them swim for about 15 minutes until they get tender.

3. When they're all softened up, drain the water and give those potatoes a cozy mash in a mixing bowl. Feel free to invite your little kitchen helpers to join the mashing party – it's a family affair!

Ingredients

- 1 ⅓ cup Pumpkin Puree
- 14 oz Russet or Yukon Potato
- 2 cups gluten-free flour, divided (keep ½ cup of flour to dust the surface where you work your gnocchi)
- 1 teaspoon Salt

Instructions– continue

4. Now, let's introduce our star ingredient – the pumpkin puree! Add it to the potato mash, along with 1 ½ cups of gluten-free flour. Mix it all up until you've got yourself a lovely, orange dough. We're basically creating edible art here.

5. To keep things precise, weigh the dough and divide it into equal portions. This way, your gnocchi will be like a well-coordinated dance troupe, all moving in perfect harmony.

6. It's time to dust your hands and the kitchen surface with the remaining ½ cup of gluten-free flour. Consider this your culinary playground.

7. Take a portion of dough and start rolling it into a ½-inch thick log or snake. Get creative with the shapes; you can even let the kids craft their own edible sculptures!

8. Trim the gnocchi pieces to the same length using a sharp knife or spatula, and place them on a tray. You're like a sculptor in an art studio, but instead of marble, you're working with delicious dough.

Optional Gnocchi Design (Italian way):

9. Feeling fancy? Let's give your gnocchi some Italian flair! Grab a fork and flip it upside down so the curved part is on top. Take a gnocchi piece and gently press it with your thumb against the fork, rolling it down. This creates those iconic gnocchi ridges that hold onto sauce like they're giving it a comforting hug.

10. Pop your beautiful creations in the freezer for about 20 minutes to firm up. In the meantime, prepare a pot of salted water and let it come to a rolling boil.

11. Once your pot is bubbling with excitement, gently place your gnocchi into the water. Cook them for just 2-3 minutes or until they joyfully float to the surface. It's like a magic show in your kitchen!

12. Use a slotted spoon to scoop out your perfectly cooked gnocchi and place them on your fanciest serving plate. They're like little culinary gems, ready to shine!

Now, here comes the fun part – you can serve these Vegan Pumpkin Gnocchi with your favourite sauce or toppings. Whether it's a classic tomato or a pesto, these pillowy, pumpkin-infused delights are ready to dazzle your taste buds.

CHEESY CHICKEN AND VEGGIE *Soup*

I was on a quest to create a soup so enchanting that even the pickiest of eaters (yes, Mia and Stella included) would ask for seconds. Our secret weapon? A gluten-free cheesy chicken and veggie soup that's as fun to make as it is to eat. Let the quest begin!

Prepare Time
15 Minutes

Cook Time
30 Minutes

Serves
4

- 2 tablespoons olive oil
- 2 boneless, skinless chicken breasts, cubed
- 1 medium onion, chopped
- 2 carrots, diced
- 2 celery stalks, diced
- 1 cup broccoli
- 4 cups gluten-free chicken broth
- 1 cup corn kernels (fresh or frozen)
- 1 teaspoon dried thyme
- 1 teaspoon garlic powder
- 2 cups shredded cheddar cheese (or a dairy-free alternative)
- Salt and pepper to taste
- Optional: gluten-free pasta or rice, cooked

Instructions

1. In a large pot, heat olive oil over medium heat. Add cubed chicken and cook until it's golden and cooked through. It's like starting a treasure hunt, where chicken is the first gem to find!

2. Add onions, carrots, and celery to the pot. Cook until the onions are translucent and the veggies are dancing in the pot.

3. Stir in zucchini, chicken broth, corn, thyme, and garlic powder. Bring the magical potion to a boil, then reduce heat and let it simmer. The magic is in the simmer!

4. Slowly stir in the cheese until it melts into a gooey, delightful blend. This is where the magic turns into a cheesy wonderland.

5. Add salt and pepper to taste. For extra heartiness, add some cooked gluten-free pasta or rice.

6. Serve hot in bowls, with each ladle full, bringing smiles and warmth.

And there we have it - a cheesy, hearty, and utterly delicious soup that conquered the hearts (and tummies) of my toughest critics. Mia and Stella, with their soup-stained grins, proclaimed it the best 'magic soup' ever. Who knew that the path to veggie appreciation was paved with cheese and laughter? Here's to warm bowls and even warmer memories! Enjoy, fellow soup wizards!

CHEESEBURGER *Soup*

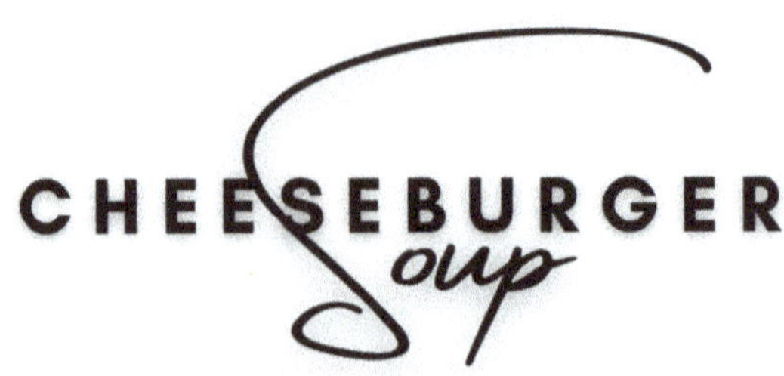

Back-to-school often means back-to-colds in our household. With sniffles and sneezes becoming the new normal, I decided to spice up our soup game with a recipe that's not just delicious but kid-approved! Presenting my hearty Cheeseburger Soup:

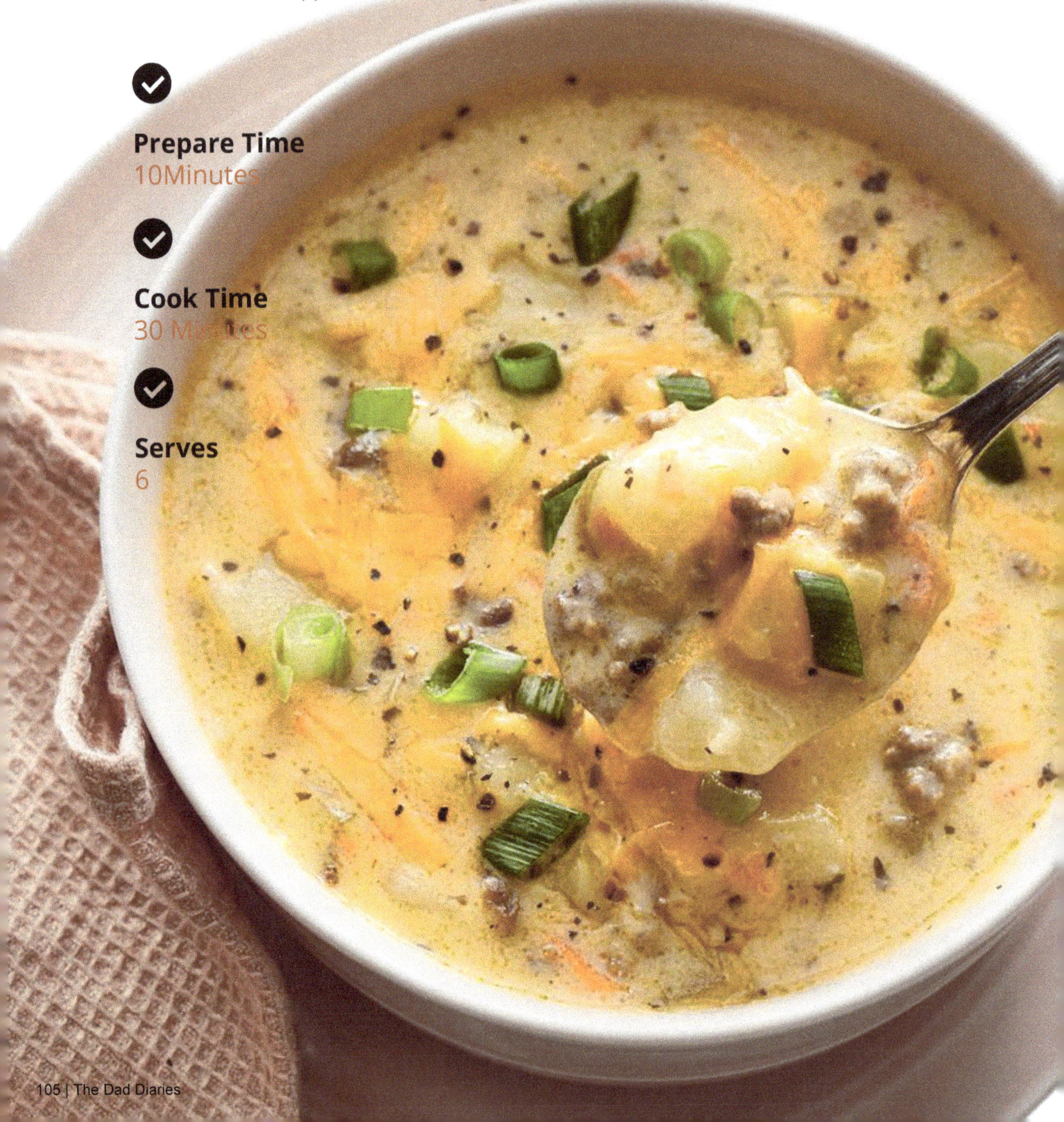

Prepare Time
10Minutes

Cook Time
30 Minutes

Serves
6

Ingredients

- 2 tablespoons olive oil
- ¾ cup sweet onion, chopped
- 3 celery stalks, chopped
- 2 carrots, shredded
- 1 pound ground beef
- 1 teaspoon Italian seasoning
- ¾ teaspoon salt
- ¼ teaspoon pepper
- 2 cups potatoes, diced
- 4 cups low-sodium chicken broth
- 2 tablespoons gluten-free flour blend
- ½ cup milk
- 1 cup cheddar cheese, shredded
- ¾ cup milk

Instructions

1. Heat up the olive oil in a pot and toss in the carrots, onions, and celery. Cook this veggie trio over medium heat for a cozy five minutes.

2. Introduce the ground beef to the party, cooking it until it boasts a beautiful brown hue. If there's an excess of grease, feel free to bid it farewell.

3. Pour in the chicken broth, add the Italian seasoning, salt, and pepper, and throw in those delightful diced potatoes. Bring this bubbling concoction to a boil, then reduce the heat and let it simmer for a tantalizing 20 minutes.

4. In a separate bowl, whisk together the gluten-free flour blend and ½ cup of milk until you have a smooth blend. Pour this mixture into the pot, stirring as you go, until your soup achieves that perfect thickness.

5. Now, it's time for the cheesy crescendo. Add the remaining ¾ cup of milk and the shredded cheddar cheese. Keep stirring until the cheese gracefully melts into the soup, creating a velvety masterpiece.

6. Ladle up this heartwarming Cheeseburger Soup and watch the smiles spread. Feel free to season it with a dash more salt and pepper, tailoring it to your taste.

This soup isn't just a treat for the taste buds; it's a comforting ally against the school-year sniffles. A hearty, wholesome bowlful that brings joy with every spoonful!

Prepare Time
15 Minutes

Bake Time
20 Minutes

Serves
6

We're about to embark on a culinary adventure to create the legendary Gluten-Free Taco Bake. The mission? To make dinner without turning the kitchen into a scene from a slapstick comedy. Spoiler alert: we failed miserably.

As I started browning the beef, Mia decided it needed a 'dance' and started shaking the pan like it was a maraca. Meanwhile, Stella, the aspiring 'cheese artist,' began crafting a cheese sculpture that would put Michelangelo to shame. Amidst the laugher and flying cheese, our Taco Bake transformed from a simple recipe to a laughter-filled family escapade. So, tie your aprons, and let's recreate the Tito family's somewhat chaotic but utterly delicious Gluten-Free Taco Bake!

Ingredients

- 1 lb ground beef
- 1 packet gluten-free taco seasoning
- 1 can black beans, drained and rinsed
- 1 cup corn (frozen or canned)
- 1 cup salsa
- 1 cup shredded cheese (cheddar or Mexican blend)
- 2 cups cooked rice
- Optional toppings: avocados, sour cream, cilantro, lime wedges

Instructions

1. Preheat the Oven: Start by heating your oven to 350°F (175°C).

2. Cook the Meat: In a large skillet, brown the ground beef over medium heat. Once cooked, drain off the excess fat.

3.Mix in the Good Stuff: Add the taco seasoning, black beans, corn, and salsa to the skillet with the beef. Stir it all together and cook for a few more minutes.

4. Layer it Up: In a baking dish, lay down a base of cooked rice. Over the rice, pour your beef and veggie mixture. Finally, sprinkle the shredded cheese on top like a cheesy blanket.

5. Bake it Away: Pop the dish in the oven for about 20 minutes. You're waiting for that cheese to melt into a gooey, golden layer of deliciousness.

6. Serve and Enjoy: Once it's bubbly and irresistible, take it out, and serve hot. Feel free to add any of the optional toppings for an extra burst of flavour.

And there you have it, folks! A dish that's not just a meal, but a memory maker. Cheers to more fun in the kitchen and a little extra cheese on top, just the way Stella likes it! A simple, scrumptious Gluten-Free Taco Bake that's bound to become a family favourite.

Prepare Time
10 Minutes

Air Fry
10 Minutes

If you haven't indulged in nachos the Francuuu way, buckle up because you're about to embark on a nacho adventure like never before. This isn't just a snack; it's a full-blown nacho fiesta that my girls can't resist, and we've turned it into a mealtime sensation. Plus, it's the ultimate crowd-pleaser for parties!

Instructions

1. Begin the nacho spectacle with a foundation of tortillas, creating the canvas for a flavourful masterpiece. Pile on the savoury ground taco beef, ensuring every bite is a taste sensation. Generously sprinkle Mexican blended cheese, setting the cheesy tone for the nacho layers. Drizzle with the vibrant salsa verde, adding a zesty kick to the fiesta. Introduce a layer of hearty black beans, adding both texture and protein goodness. Crown this base layer with another round of tortillas, preparing for the nacho symphony.

2. Dive into another round of cheesy bliss with a layer of Mexican blended cheese. Add pickled jalapeños for that perfect tangy twist. Sprinkle a melody of raw white onions, tomatoes, and peppers, creating a colourful mosaic of flavours. Another layer of tortillas adds a satisfying crunch to the nacho crescendo. Top it off with yet another generous layer of cheese, ensuring a gooey delight in every bite.

3. Elevate the nacho experience with more tomatoes, salsa verde, and black beans. Seal the deal with a final layer of tortillas, creating the pinnacle of nacho perfection. Crown this summit with an encore of ground taco beef and a thick, irresistible layer of Mexican blended cheese. Sprinkle freshness with jalapeños for that extra kick.

4. Into the air fryer at 400 degrees for 10 minutes, where the magic happens. Watch as the layers meld, the cheese bubbles and the aroma of nacho excellence fills the air.

6. No nacho extravaganza is complete without dollops of cool sour cream, creamy guacamole, and a little more salsa verde.

The moment of truth! Dive into this towering nacho creation that's not just a dish but a flavour symphony. Every layer brings a new dimension of taste and texture. Prepare for an "Oh my god!" moment. Whether it's a family meal or a party sensation, Nachos Alla Francuuu is a fiesta on a plate that promises to elevate your nacho experience to legendary heights. ¡Viva la nacho revolución!

Ingredients

- Tortillas
- Ground taco beef
- Mexican blended cheese
- Salsa verde
- Black beans
- Pickled jalapenos
- Raw white onions
- Tomatoes
- Peppers
- Olives
- Fresh jalapenos
- Sour cream
- Guacamole

TACO-STUFFED *Bell Peppers*

Prepare Time
20 Minutes

Bake
30 Minutes

Serves
4

Let me tell you how our taco night toke a wild turn into uncharted territories! Here's the scene: it's Taco Tuesday, and the excitement is palpable. But wait - Mia and Stella, declare a taco rebellion! "No more shells!" they chant, wielding spatulas like sceptres. In a flash of inspiration (and a pinch of dad genius), I present our latest culinary escapade: Taco-Stuffed Bell Peppers. It's tacos, but not as you know them!

- 4 large bell peppers, any color
- 1 lb ground turkey or beef
- 1 packet gluten-free taco seasoning
- 1 can black beans, drained and rinsed
- 1 cup corn kernels
- 1 cup shredded cheddar cheese
- ½ cup salsa
- 1 tablespoon olive oil
- Salt and pepper to taste
- Optional toppings: sour cream, avocado, fresh cilantro

1. Start by slicing the tops off the bell peppers and removing the seeds. It's like carving mini pumpkins, but with less spooky and more yummy.

2. In a skillet, heat the olive oil and brown the meat. Stir in taco seasoning, beans, corn, and salsa. Let the rebellion begin!

3. Spoon the meat mixture into each bell pepper, like filling treasure chests with golden taco booty.

4. Sprinkle the tops with cheese, because everything's better with a cheesy hat.

5. Pop them in the oven at 375°F for about 25-30 minutes, or until the peppers are tender and the cheese is bubbly.

6. Top with a dollop of sour cream, slices of avocado, and a sprinkle of cilantro. It's a fiesta on a plate!

And there you have it - a twist on taco night that quelled the great taco rebellion in the Monteleone-Tito household. Mia and Stella, our once-rebellious chefs, are now the biggest fans of these colorful, stuffed wonders. "Papa, we should start a pepper rebellion every week!" they giggle, their plates wiped clean. Mission accomplished: bell peppers have been officially taco-fied!

Enjoy your own family's taco night with a twist, and remember, in the kitchen, a little rebellion now and then is a tasty thing!

Prepare Time
10 Minutes

Bake Time
15 Minutes

Serves
4

If there's one dish that brings a fiesta to our table, it's these scrumptious Gluten-Free Enchiladas. Packed with flavour and oozing with cheesy goodness, they're a crowd-pleaser that even my littlest critics devour with gusto.

Now, let's get this fiesta started:

Ingredients

- 1 can gluten-free enchilada sauce
- 12 gluten-free corn tortillas
- 2 cups cooked chicken, shredded or diced
- 1 cup cheese, shredded (cheddar, Mozzarella)
- (Optional, but highly recommended: cilantro, beans, corn, or any of your other favourite fillings)

Instructions

1. Preheat the oven to 400°F. We're about to turn up the heat in the kitchen!

2. To prep your tortillas, wrap them in a paper towel and give them a 30-second spin in the microwave. This warms them up and makes them flexible, ready to cradle our flavourful filling.

3. Now, let's set the saucey stage. Spread about ½ cup of enchilada sauce over the bottom of a microwave-safe rectangle casserole dish. This will be the foundation for our flavour-packed creation.

4. In a mixing bowl, it's time for our chicken to shine. Mix it with any additional fillings you fancy and about 1 cup of that delectable enchilada sauce. This mixture is the heart and soul of our enchiladas, so go ahead and get creative!

5. Take each tortilla and give it a little dip in the remaining enchilada sauce. This ensures that every bite is bursting with that authentic enchilada taste. Fill each tortilla with 2 ½-3 tablespoons of the chicken filling, then roll it up and place it in the pan, seam side down. Repeat this delicious process with the remaining tortillas and filling.

6. There might be a little enchilada sauce left – don't let it go to waste! Spread it lovingly over the top of our enchiladas. This sauce is what's going to make our dish truly spectacular.

7. It's time to bring on the cheese! Sprinkle that glorious shredded goodness over the top of our enchiladas. This is where the magic happens.

8. Into the oven they go, for about 10-15 minutes. Keep a watchful eye – we're looking for golden, bubbly perfection.

And there you have it, amigos! Your Cheesy Chicken Fiesta: Gluten-Free Enchiladas are ready to steal the spotlight. Serve them up with a side of laughter and good company for a mealtime experience that's truly memorable. Enjoy!

GLUTEN-FREE
Pie Crust

Finally, a gluten-free pie crust that's a breeze to make, easy to roll, refuses to crack, and tastes downright fantastic! No more compromising on texture or flavour – this step-by-step recipe will guide you to create the most tender, buttery, gluten-free pie crust that's a game-changer. It's a dough that comes together swiftly, is as supple as a yoga master, and rolls out like a dream. Perfect for both sweet and savoury creations!

Prepare Time
20 Minutes

Instructions

1. In a food processor, toss in the flour, sugar, and salt. Give it a few pulses to mingle the ingredients.

2. Place those cold, cubed butter pieces on the flour. Pulse again until the butter is pea-sized, and the mix is a bit shaggy.

3. Add the cold mashed potato to the mix. Another round of pulsing until it's all nicely combined, keeping that shaggy vibe.

4. With the food processor in action, stream in the ice water until the dough starts cozying up. Unplug the processor.

5. Use your hands or a spatula to bring the dough to life. Turn the food processor container upside down onto a floured pastry mat.

6. Knead the dough about 3-5 times in each direction. Form it into a smooth disk, then roll it out into a generous 12-14 inch circle. Size doesn't matter, but bigger is better.

7. Gently lift the pie crust and slide your pie pan underneath, letting the dough hang over the edges.

8. For Fluting: Use your thumb and index finger to create a scalloped masterpiece.
For Crimping: Let your hands gently gather the dough into a rim, then press down with the tines of a fork for that professional touch.

9. If some edges are too rebellious, trim them a bit. This dough is versatile – it understands.

10. Now, this gluten-free wonder is ready for your favourite sweet or savoury pie! Because pie shouldn't discriminate against gluten, and neither should you. Enjoy your effortlessly fabulous pie crust!

Ingredients

- 1¼ cups gluten-free all-purpose flour
- 1 tablespoon granulated sugar
- ⅛ teaspoon salt
- 6 tablespoons COLD butter cut into small cubes
- ¼ cup cooked, mashed, cold potato
- ¼ cup ice water

Prepare your taste buds for a journey into savoury bliss with this gluten-free Spinach, Goat Cheese & Sun-Dried Tomato Quiche. Creamy, flavour-packed, and crowned with a gluten-free pie crust, this quiche is not just a meal – it's an experience. Perfect for lazy brunches, festive breakfasts, or making your meal prep game strong!

Prepare Time
20 Minutes

Bake
40 Minutes

SPINACH, GOAT CHEESE
&
Sun-Dried Tomato Quiche

Ingredients

- 1 gluten-free pie crust (store bought or go to the previous recipe to make your own)
- 1 tablespoon olive oil
- 2-3 cloves garlic, minced
- 1/2 cup yellow onion, chopped
- 3 cups fresh spinach, packed
- 5 large eggs
- 1 cup whole milk
- 1/2 cup sun-dried tomatoes in oil, drained and chopped
- 4 ounces goat cheese, crumbled or chopped
- 1 tablespoon fresh rosemary, chopped
- Salt & pepper to taste

Instructions

1.Preheat the oven to 350 degrees F and ensure your gluten-free pie crust is partially baked – because a golden crust is the canvas for this masterpiece.

2. In a medium skillet, let the olive oil dance over medium heat. Add onions and sauté for 5 minutes until tender and translucent. Introduce garlic, sauté for about 30 seconds until the aroma hits you. Add spinach and cook until wilted (3-5 minutes). Remove this flavourful mix from heat and set it aside. Pro tip: Save a few pieces of spinach, goat cheese, and tomatoes for the quiche's red carpet moment.

3. In a large mixing bowl, whisk eggs and milk until they become the dynamic duo. Stir in sun-dried tomatoes, goat cheese, rosemary, and the onion/spinach mix. Season with salt and pepper. Pro tip: If your sun-dried tomatoes pack a salty punch, go easy on the additional salt.

4. Pour this egg symphony into the prepared pie crust. If you saved some spinach, goat cheese, and sun-dried tomatoes, let them gracefully adorn the quiche. Cover the crust edges with foil to shield them from the baking spotlight. Bake at 350°F for approximately 40-45 minutes or until the quiche achieves a golden brown hue and a centred, set perfection. Check at 30-35 minutes – if stardom is approaching too fast, gently cover the entire quiche with foil for the final act.

5. Let the quiche bask in its glory for 5 minutes before serving – because every star needs a moment.

Get ready to savour the Marvellous Medley of Flavours – where spinach, goat cheese, and sun-dried tomatoes unite in a gluten-free symphony of taste!

Snacks

Snack time: that glorious daily intermission between meals where our adorable little ones magically transform into professional negotiators. "Can I have a cookie?" "How about some chips?" Sound familiar? It's like they've suddenly enrolled in a crash course on bargaining tactics, and I'll admit, sometimes they're good enough to make me reconsider the cookie ban.

Welcome to the Snack-tionary chapter, where we navigate the wild world of munchies with all the finesse of a ringmaster at the snack circus. Whether you're dealing with post-school munchies, the dreaded "I'm bored" snack request, or just the need to hold them off until dinner, I've got you covered. We'll be diving into snacks that aren't just about keeping tummies full but about creating those little moments of joy—like Stella's giggle when she gets the "extra crunchy one" or Mia's grin when she sprinkles cinnamon just right on her apple slices.

So join me on this flavorful journey through crispy, crunchy, and downright munchable treats. Let's transform those desperate snack requests into opportunities to laugh, create, and connect. After all, when it comes to snacks, we're all just one bag of chips away from being snack-chefs extraordinaire, and turning a simple moment into a memory worth savoring.

Nutella Brownies

Prepare Time
10 Minutes

Cook Time
20 Minutes

Serves
6

Alright, parents, lean in close because we're about to whip up some Nutella Brownie Bites so fast, your kids won't even have time to ask, 'Are we there yet?' Yeah, you heard that right—these little chunks of chocolate bliss are about to become your secret weapon. Think about it: whipping up a mouth-watering treat quicker than your toddler can spot a loophole in your "no more snacks" rule. Get ready to don your apron like a superhero cape, because these brownie bites are going to make you the legend of snack time. Prepare for some serious parent points!

Ingredients

- 2 large eggs
- 1 cup Nutella

Instructions

1. Preheat the oven to 350°F. Make sure your oven rack is in the middle because we're aiming for brownie perfection here.

2. Grab your muffin trays and give them a quick spray with cooking spray or lightly grease them with a touch of oil. We're making life easy and mess-free, just like parenting should be (in theory).

3. In a mixing bowl, whisk those eggs until they're light and fluffy. Think of it as your mini workout for the day. This will take about 5 min with a mixer or a bit longer if you're using elbow grease.

4. Warm up that Nutella in a microwave-safe bowl. Pop it in the microwave on high for 1 minute, stirring every 15 seconds until it's velvety and smooth.

5. Now, the fun part—mixing the eggs and Nutella. Pour your fluffy eggs into the Nutella and give it a good stir. No need for perfection here; we're keeping it real.

6. Spoon this delightful mixture into your muffin trays. Fill 'em up, and don't worry about perfection; rustic is in, trust me.

7. Pop those trays in the preheated oven and bake for about 20-25 minutes. Keep an eye on them—they're ready when they look all puffed up and a toothpick inserted into the middle comes out clean. It's like magic happening in your oven.

8. Once they're done, let them cool a bit (if you can resist the temptation), then pop them out of the trays. Nutella Brownie Bites are perfect for little hands and your big appetite.

Prepare Time
10 Minutes

Bake Time
10 Minutes

Serves
22 Cookies

We're diving headfirst into the world of gluten-free goodness with these Peanut Butter Chocolate Chip Cookies that are so easy that even a sleep-deprived parent can handle them. With just 4 simple ingredients, you'll have a plate of heavenly cookies in no time. Here's how the cookie crumbles:

Ingredients

- 2 cups of peanut butter (or any smooth nut butter you fancy)
- 2 eggs
- 1 cup of brown sugar
- 1 cup of chocolate chips (because I believe in a generous dose of chocolate therapy)

Instructions

1. Preheat your oven to 175°C/350°F, and line a baking tray with parchment paper. Consider this your cookie superhero cape—no sticky messes to clean up later.

2. In a mixing bowl, beat 2 eggs (like you're beating the early morning blues), then mix in 2 cups of peanut butter. I prefer the Kirkland brand—it's a little less sweet and slightly healthier, but any smooth nut butter will do. Add 1 cup of brown sugar to the mix, and keep stirring until it's smooth yet thick. It's cookie-making cardio!

3. Softly introduce the chocolate chips to the party. Gently fold them into the peanut butter mix, like you're welcoming old friends.

4. Time to get your hands dirty (figuratively). Scoop out spoonfuls of the cookie dough and roll them into balls. Channel your inner child, and make them as big or as small as you like.

5. Place these doughy wonders on the prepared baking tray. If you prefer your cookies a bit flatter, give them a gentle press with a fork. But, we've got a secret—Joseph's little critics love the ball shape, so it's your call.

6. Bake these babies in the oven for about 10 minutes. While they're baking, resist the urge to sneak a taste because patience is a virtue (and warm cookies crumble, remember?).

7. We can't stress this enough: DO NOT attempt to move them until they're cool. Patience, my friend, patience. These cookies need to chill and solidify, just like a parent's sanity after a long day.

There you have it, Dad's No-Fail Peanut Butter Choco-Chip Delights—a batch of gluten-free, melt-in-your-mouth cookies that'll have your family screaming for more. So go ahead, whip up a plate of these, and savour the delicious chaos of parenting, one cookie at a time.

DAD'S PEANUT BUTTER
Oat Dream Cups

You won't believe how easy and scrumptious these treats are! Picture this: rich and creamy peanut butter, the wholesome goodness of oats, and a decadent chocolate topping, all in a convenient little cup. We've named them "Dad's Peanut Butter Oat Dream Cups" because they're the stuff dreams are made of. Whip up a batch, pop them in the freezer, and you'll have a delicious snack ready whenever you fancy a sweet indulgence.

Ingredients

For the Cups:

- 1 cup rolled oats
- 1/4 cup almond flour
- 1 cup natural peanut butter
- 1/2 cup maple syrup (or honey)
- 1 tsp vanilla extract
- 1/2 tsp salt

For the Chocolate Topping:

- 1/2 cup chocolate chips
- 2 tbsp peanut butter
- A sprinkle of flaky salt

Instructions

For the Cups:

1. In a medium-sized bowl, mix together the rolled oats, almond flour, peanut butter, maple syrup (or honey), vanilla extract, and salt. Combine everything until it's a heavenly, sticky mixture.

2. Line a muffin tin with liners and evenly distribute the mixture. Flatten the tops as best as you can, making them look irresistible.

3. Now, pop that muffin tin into the freezer for at least 2 hours. We know it's tough to wait, but it's totally worth it!

For the Chocolate Topping:

1. In a small pot over low heat, melt the chocolate chips and peanut butter together, stirring constantly until they form a smooth and dreamy blend.

2. Take the muffin tin out of the freezer and generously drizzle about 1-2 tablespoons of the chocolate mix on top of each cup. Make it look as tempting as possible.

3. Sprinkle a dash of flaky salt on each cup to give them that extra oomph, and then back into the freezer they go for another hour.

4. Once they've set, store these heavenly cups in an airtight container in the freezer. Whenever you crave a delightful snack, grab one and savor the sweet and salty perfection!

These Dad's Peanut Butter Oat Dream Cups are not just a treat; they're a mini-escape to indulgence town!

HOMEMADE
Twix Bars

I remember my childhood fascination with candy bars, especially the iconic Twix. Those layers of shortbread, caramel, and chocolate had a magical appeal. Now, as a dad with an eye on health, I wanted to create a version that's not only delicious but also better for us. These homemade peanut butter Twix bars are the result, and they've become a family favourite. With a shortbread base, a luscious peanut butter caramel middle, and a dark chocolate topping, these bars are naturally sweetened, vegan, and gluten-free.

Prepare Time
30 Minutes

Bake Time
15 Minutes

Serves
16

Ingredients

For the shortbread base:
- 1 ½ cups almond flour
- 3 tbsp melted and cooled coconut oil
- 2 tbsp pure maple syrup
- 1 tsp vanilla extract
- ¼ tsp salt

For the peanut butter layer:
- ⅔ cup peanut butter
- 1/3 cup pure maple syrup
- 1/4 cup coconut oil
- 1 tsp vanilla extract
- 1/4 tsp sea salt

For the chocolate layer:
- 3/4 cup chocolate chips
- 1 tbsp coconut oil

Instructions

1. Preheat the oven to 350 degrees F. Line an 8x8 inch square pan with parchment paper. The choice of the right-sized pan is crucial; using a 9x9 inch might make the bars too thin.

Note: I've learned from experience that the size of the pan can affect the texture and thickness of the bars. My first attempt ended up too thin, and the layers weren't as indulgent as I had hoped. That's why the 8x8-inch pan is essential for the perfect Twix experience.

2. In a medium bowl, combine the almond flour, coconut oil, maple syrup, vanilla extract, and salt. Mix with a fork until it forms a thick, crumbly texture. Press this shortbread mixture evenly into the pan using your fingers. Bake for 10 minutes. Allow the crust to cool for 10 minutes before adding the caramel layer.

3. Now, for the peanut butter caramel layer: In a medium pot, add the peanut butter, maple syrup, coconut oil, vanilla extract, and sea salt. Heat it over medium-low for about 2 minutes until the caramel starts to bubble slightly, stirring frequently. Pour this over the slightly cooled crust.

4. Place the pan in the fridge for at least 30 minutes to 1 hour until the peanut butter layer hardens. If patience is not your virtue, you can speed up the process by placing it in the freezer for 15-20 minutes.

5. After the peanut butter layer has set, it's time for the chocolate layer. Melt the chocolate chips and coconut oil in a microwave-safe bowl on high in 30-second increments, stirring in between until the chocolate is completely melted. Alternatively, you can melt the chocolate and coconut oil in a small saucepan over low heat.

6. Pour the melted chocolate over the caramel layer and tilt the pan side-to-side to distribute it evenly. Place the pan back in the fridge for at least 20 minutes until the chocolate is completely hardened and the bars have cooled.

7. Remove the bars from the pan and cut them into 16 bars that resemble Twix bars. To do this, cut the entire pan of bars in half and then cut each half into 8 (1-inch) bars, not squares. This way, you'll end up with 16 bars that truly capture the spirit of Twix. Enjoy! Keep the bars covered in the fridge until you're ready to serve.

Chocolate Coconut Patties

Prepare Time
10 Minutes

Ready to whip up something that doesn't involve burning water or setting off the smoke alarm? Great! Let's dive into making some gluten-free chocolate coconut patties that are so easy, even I managed not to mess them up – and that's saying something!

- 1 cup unsweetened shredded coconut (because who needs extra sugar when life is already sweet with kids, right?)

- 3 1/2 tbsp pure maple syrup, honey, or agave (whichever one you can find in the pantry chaos)

- 2 tbsp virgin coconut oil (not to be confused with the motor oil in the garage)

- 1/2 tsp pure vanilla extract (the secret weapon)

- 1/8 tsp salt (just a pinch, like the one you use when your kid says they cleaned their room)

- 3 oz chocolate chips (for that 'life is better with chocolate' philosophy)

Instructions

1. Grab your food processor or blender. Yes, the one gathering dust in the corner. Throw in the coconut, sweetener of choice, coconut oil, vanilla extract, and salt. Hit the button and watch it go. It's like a culinary mosh pit in there!

2. Once you've got a mixture that sticks together better than a toddler to their favorite toy, it's time to get your hands dirty. Line a plate with wax or parchment paper (because who needs extra cleaning, right?) and form the mixture into patties. If it's stickier than a melted lollipop on a car seat, chill it in the freezer for a bit.

3. Melt the chocolate chips gently. If you're feeling fancy, stir in that optional teaspoon of oil for extra smoothness – it's like giving your patties a chocolate jacuzzi.

4. Dip the patties into the melted chocolate. It's okay if it gets messy – that's half the fun. Then, back into the freezer they go until they're firmer than your stance on not sharing your secret snack stash.

5. Once they're set, serve them up! They can hang out at room temperature for a bit, much like your kids when you tell them it's bedtime.

And there you have it, folks! Dad's no-fuss, gluten-free chocolate coconut patties. Perfect for when you want to impress but only have ten minutes of peace. Enjoy your culinary victory – you've earned it!

Pear Delights

Prepare Time
15 Minutes

Bake Time
35 Minutes

Serves
8

Let's embark on a culinary adventure that's as fun to make as it is to eat—Introducing "Pear-fectly Baked Pear Delights!" These delightful treats are a breeze to prepare, and they'll have your taste buds dancing with joy. So, gather your ingredients and let's get started:

Ingredients

- 4 ripe pears
- 1/2 cup melted butter
- 1 tablespoon cinnamon sugar
- 1 cup GF rolled oats
- 1/2 cup finely chopped almonds
- 1/3 cup brown sugar
- 1 teaspoon ground cinnamon
- 1 teaspoon sea salt
- honey for drizzling

Instructions

1. Begin by preheating your trusty oven to a toasty 400º. As it warms up, you'll start the pear-fect transformation of these ripe pears. Halve them and scoop out just enough from the center to create a cozy nest for our oatmeal crumble. Then, brush the insides of the pears with 2 tablespoons of melted butter and sprinkle them with a touch of cinnamon sugar. It's like giving each pear a sugary hug.

2. In a medium-sized bowl, bring together the stars of our oatmeal crumble show: oats, finely chopped almonds, brown sugar, cinnamon, and a pinch of salt. Now, pour the remaining melted butter into the mix and give it all a good toss until everything is wonderfully coated. This is where the magic begins.

3. Spoon this delicious oatmeal crumble into the waiting pear halves. Imagine it as a cozy bed for our pear guests. They're in for a treat!

4. Slide your pear-fect creations into the preheated oven and let them bake until the pears become soft and tender. This takes around 35 to 40 minutes, during which your kitchen will be filled with the irresistible aroma of cinnamon and baked goodness.

5. Once they're ready, drizzle some honey on top and crown these pear delights with a small scoop of vanilla ice cream. The contrast of warm, baked pears and cold, creamy ice cream is a symphony of flavours and temperatures that's sure to delight your taste buds.

There you have it, "Pear-fectly Baked Pear Delights"! A dessert that's not only fun to say but even more fun to eat. Enjoy these pear-fect treats warm and savour the pear-fectly sweet, cinnamon-kissed moments they bring to your kitchen!

Looking for a guilt-free dessert that's low on sugar but high on flavor? Well, you've stumbled upon a true gem! This Custardy Greek Yogurt Cake is a delightful treat that's perfect for those looking to satisfy their sweet tooth without the sugar overload.

Ingredients

- 1½ cups 5% Greek yogurt
- 4 eggs
- 5 tablespoons tapioca flour (or corn starch)

Optional Toppings:
- Fresh Fruit
- Honey
- Maple Syrup
- Powdered Sugar
- Shaved Chocolate
- Lemon Zest
- Orange Zest

Optional Flavour Adventures:
- A splash of vanilla extract
- A sprinkle of cinnamon

Instructions

1. Preheat your oven to 350°F (175°C). Spray your 6-inch round springform pan with oil and line it with parchment paper. Pro tip: scrunch the paper before lining the pan; it'll shape better.

2. In a large bowl, add the Greek yogurt and whisk in the eggs. Stir until the batter is silky smooth. Next, sift in your cornstarch (or tapioca flour) and whisk until it's fully incorporated and the batter remains smooth.

3. Transfer the batter to your prepped pan and bake for about 1 hour or until the top is puffed up and golden brown. As it cools, the top will deflate – that's exactly what we want.

4. Allow the cake to cool for 30 minutes in the pan. Don't remove it during this process. Then, transfer the cake to the fridge and let it cool for at least 2 hours to set. Remove the cake from the fridge 15 minutes before serving.

Optional & Recommended Toppings: Since this recipe is sugar-free, you can get creative with your toppings. Consider adding some fresh berries, drizzling honey, dusting with powdered sugar, grating chocolate, or zesting some citrus fruits for that extra zing.

Indulge in this delightful, custardy creation that's as satisfying as it is guilt-free. It's the perfect treat for those who want to enjoy dessert without the sugar rush.

Let's take a little break from the regular and dive into a world of dessert magic. We're about to whip up some scrumptious Apple Pie Ice Cream, and guess what? It's gluten and dairy-free, making it a fantastic treat for everyone to enjoy! Here's how we do it:

Ingredients

- 3 small apples, freshly sliced
- 1 can of coconut cream (13.5 oz) – our dairy-free superstar
- 2 tsp of heavenly apple pie spice
- ¼ cup of pure maple syrup (or the golden goodness of raw honey)

Instructions

1. First things first, let's give those apples a good wash and slice them up. We're getting ready for a fruity fiesta!

2. Now, gather all your wonderful ingredients in a blender. That's the sliced apples, the luscious coconut cream, the aromatic apple pie spice, and the sweet maple syrup (or honey, if that's your thing).

3. Time to blend it all together until you reach that silky-smooth, creamy consistency that screams "Apple Pie Ice Cream."

4. Grab an ice cube tray – your trusty accomplice in this dessert caper. Transfer your delightful mixture into those little cube compartments, getting them all snug and cozy.

5. Now, patience is a virtue. Pop that tray into the freezer for 1-2 hours. We want those cubes to harden up, getting ready for their transformation into ice cream.

6. Once they're appropriately chilled, it's blending time once more. Pop those frozen cubes back into your blender and give them a whirl until you achieve that perfect creamy texture. You might need to do a little scraping down the sides for the ultimate smoothness.

7. For an extra touch of delight, how about adding some crushed gluten-free graham crackers on top? Or go wild with your favourite toppings – it's your ice cream kingdom, after all.

And there you have it – a glorious, gluten and dairy-free Apple Pie Ice Cream that'll make everyone's taste buds do a happy dance. So, scoop up a bowl, savour every bite, and let the dessert dreams begin!

Apple Pie Bites

If you're searching for a gluten-free treat that embodies the essence of apple pie in every bite, then you've landed on the perfect page. These Apple Pie Bits are incredibly delicious and easy to make. The best part? They're kid-friendly, making them a delightful addition to your family's snack repertoire.

Prepare Time
15 Minutes

Cool Time
1 hour

Serves
12

- 2 apples, chopped
- 1 cup almond flour
- 1/2 cup natural peanut butter
- 1/4 cup maple syrup
- 1 tsp vanilla extract
- 1 tsp apple pie spice (or cinnamon for a classic twist)
- (Optional) Melted dark chocolate for that extra touch of sweetness

Instructions

1. In a culinary symphony of flavours, combine the chopped apples, almond flour, natural peanut butter, maple syrup, vanilla extract, and the essence of apple pie with the apple pie spice (or cinnamon if you prefer). Let the ingredients waltz together in a bowl.

2. Gently scoop this delectable mixture into muffin molds, creating bite-sized pieces of apple pie joy. It's like having your own little apple pie party in the palm of your hand.

3. To elevate the sweetness factor, drizzle some melted chocolate over the top. This is where your dessert transforms into a masterpiece – a miniature version of apple pie that will make your taste buds dance with delight.

4. Let these mini creations chill in the refrigerator, allowing all the flavours to harmonize into a perfect symphony of taste. It's like the calm before the dessert storm.

5. Once that chocolate has solidified into a sweet crescendo, it's time to savour each and every bite.

These Apple Pie Bits are not just gluten-free delights; they're moments of pure, unadulterated enjoyment. Don't forget to share the love with your family. It's also a wonderful opportunity to get the kids involved in creating these delectable treats, building memories that will last a lifetime. Remember, when you embark on this culinary adventure, you're not just cooking – you're crafting moments of happiness with every bite.

CHOCOLATE Banana Bark

I'll never forget the time I stumbled upon this delectable Chocolate Banana Bark in a charming little mom-and-pop trattoria nestled in the heart of Tuscany. It was an unexpected twist on traditional snacking that immediately won my heart. As I savoured the sweet combination of bananas, creamy peanut butter, and rich dark chocolate, I knew I had to recreate this delightful treat and share it with all the snack enthusiasts out there.

Now, I'm excited to pass on the recipe that brings me back to that cozy trattoria, offering you a chance to unleash your inner chocolatier and savour a delicious fusion of flavours that's bound to delight taste buds of all ages. This Chocolate Banana Bark is not only easy to make but also a guaranteed crowd-pleaser. So, let's dive into the recipe and create some sweet memories!

Prepare Time
5 Minutes

Chill Time
40 Minutes

Serves
8

Ingredients

- 2 bananas
- 1/4 cup creamy peanut butter
- 1/3 cup dark chocolate chips
- Flaky sea salt
- Optional: chopped nuts or dried fruit

Instructions

1. Line a baking sheet with parchment paper or a silicone baking mat. This will prevent the banana from sticking to the sheet and make for easy removal later.

2. Cut up the bananas into 1-inch slices and add them to the prepared baking sheet. Make sure all banana slices are touching.

3. Cover with another piece of parchment paper. Using the bottom of a glass, press down on the banana pieces so they become one layer.

4. Add the melted peanut butter over the banana layer and place it in the freezer for 30 minutes until it hardens.

5. In a microwave-safe bowl or using a double boiler, melt the dark chocolate or semisweet chocolate until it becomes smooth and glossy. Stir occasionally to ensure even melting. Add in the coconut oil.

6. Once the banana and peanut butter layer has hardened, add the melted chocolate over the top. Sprinkle with coarse sea salt and return it to the freezer to harden again.

7. Once solidified, break up the chocolate peanut butter banana bark into pieces. Enjoy!

This Chocolate Banana Bark is a delightful treat that's easy to make and even easier to enjoy. Whether you're savouring it alone or sharing it with friends and family, it's a reminder that the most cherished recipes can come from the unlikeliest of places. Bon appetito!

✓

Prepare Time
5 Minutes

✓

Bake Time
15 Minutes

✓

Serves
6 Cookies

Get ready to be enchanted by the magic of pumpkin in these gluten-free Pumpkin Magic Cookies. They're a delightful treat that combines the warmth of pumpkin spice with the richness of cashews and coconut flakes. Here's how to create these enchanting cookies:

Ingredients

- 1 1/2 cups cashews
- 1 1/2 cups unsweetened coconut flakes
- 3/4 cup chocolate chips
- 1 cup GF graham cracker crust
- 3/4 can (11-12 oz) condensed coconut milk
- 2 tbsp pumpkin puree
- 2 tsp pumpkin spice

Instructions

1. Begin your magical journey by preheating your oven to 350°F. We're about to create a little dessert enchantment!

2. In a mystical bowl, combine the cashews, unsweetened coconut flakes, chocolate chips, GF graham cracker crust, and the essence of pumpkin with the pumpkin puree and pumpkin spice. Let these ingredients dance together until they are well coated with the enchanting coconut condensed milk.

3. With a bit of wizardry, spoon large portions of this mixture onto a parchment-lined baking sheet. But be cautious; these magic cookies like their space, as the coconut condensed milk has a tendency to spread its charm.

4. Bake these enchanting morsels for 15-16 minutes or until they take on a golden hue. The aroma alone will have your senses spellbound.

5. Once these mystical creations emerge from the oven, take a moment to observe. If the coconut condensed milk has ventured too far, use a small bowl or spoon to gently coax it back towards the cookie. These are magical cookies, but we must respect their boundaries.

6. Now comes the real test of patience – do not touch the cookies for around 10 minutes. Allow them to cool and let the condensed milk harden. This will seal the magic within, ensuring you experience the full enchantment with every bite.

These Pumpkin Magic Cookies are not only gluten-free wonders but also the perfect companions for a cozy evening or an autumn gathering. So, why wait? Create some culinary magic and indulge in the spellbinding taste of these gluten-free delights.

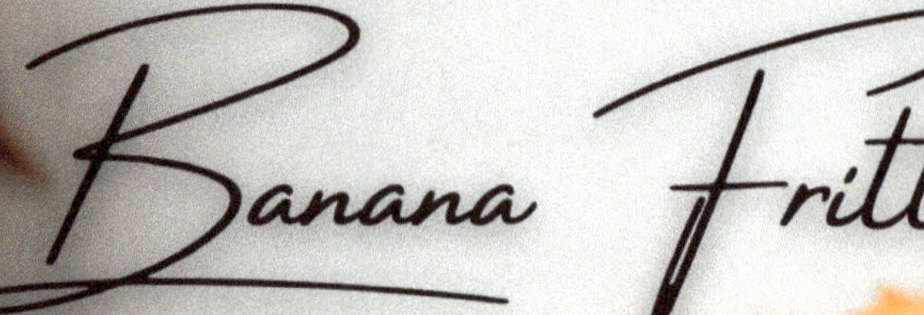

Prepare Time
15 Minutes

Bake Time
10 Minutes

Serves
6

Discover the exotic flavours of Thailand with these Coconut Coated Banana Fritters, a delightful recipe I stumbled upon during my pre-parenthood adventures in Bangkok. These fritters feature ripe banana slices, dipped in a gluten-free batter, coated in shredded coconut, and fried to a crisp, golden perfection. Drizzled with maple syrup and accompanied by a tangy lime wedge, these fritters offer a mouthwatering taste of Thailand's bustling street food culture, making them a delectable addition to your family's gluten-free culinary repertoire.

Ingredients

- 2 ripe bananas
- ½ cup gluten-free all-purpose (plain) flour, plus extra for coating
- ¼ cup cornstarch (corn flour)
- ½ tsp baking powder
- ½ tsp salt
- ¼ tsp cinnamon
- ⅓ cup (120g) cold sparkling water
- 1 ½ cups shredded coconut
- Vegetable oil for frying
- Maple syrup
- 1 lime

Instructions

1. Begin by scoring the banana skins, removing them, and cutting off the ends (perfect for a quick snack). Slice each banana into two pieces, then split each piece into two slices.

2. In a mixing bowl, combine cornstarch, gluten-free flour, baking powder, cinnamon, and salt. Set this mixture aside.

3. On one plate, place the shredded coconut, and on another plate, spread some gluten-free all-purpose (plain) flour for coating.

4. While preparing the coating, pour vegetable oil into a deep pan and heat it to 340°F (170°C).

5. To create the batter, add very cold sparkling water to your dry mix, stirring until well combined. Be sure not to overmix. (Keep the batter as cold as possible, so prepare it just before frying.)

6. Coat the banana pieces in flour, dip them into the batter, and allow any excess to drip off. Then, place them in the shredded coconut, pressing gently to ensure the coconut sticks to the batter.

7. Fry four pieces at a time in the heated oil, deep-frying them until they turn a delightful golden brown and become crispy. After frying, drain them on a cooling rack to remove excess oil.

8. Serve these fritters hot, drizzled with maple syrup and accompanied by a zesty lime cheek or wedge. For an extra treat, pair them with a scoop of creamy vanilla ice cream!

Transport your family's taste buds to the vibrant streets of Thailand with these delightful Coconut Coated Banana Fritters – a gluten-free culinary adventure that's perfect for breakfast, dessert, or anytime you crave a little taste of Thailand.

CHOCOLATE-DIPPED *Banana Pops*

Transform ordinary bananas into a mouthwatering dessert with my recipe for Chocolate-Dipped Banana Pops. These delightful treats are delicious to eat and fun to make - making them the perfect option for a mid-day snack or a creative activity to do with family and friends. It's no surprise that these banana pops are Stella's ultimate indulgence - she loves the combination of sweet, ripe bananas and decadent chocolate coating, creating a treat that is both satisfyingly simple and irresistibly tasty. So, gather your loved ones and get ready to elevate your snacking game with these delectable banana pops!

Prepare Time
120 minutes

Freeze Time
20 Minutes

Serves
8 banana pops

1. Peel the bananas and cut them in half. Insert a popsicle stick or skewer into each banana half, creating a banana pop. Place them on a baking sheet lined with parchment paper and freeze for about 1 hour.

2. In a microwave-safe bowl, combine chocolate chips and coconut oil. Microwave in 30-second intervals, stirring in between, until the chocolate is smooth and melted.

3. Dip each frozen banana pop into the melted chocolate, twirling it to coat evenly. Let the kids sprinkle their favourite toppings over the chocolate. It's like painting but way tastier!

4. Place the chocolate-dipped bananas back on the parchment paper and freeze again until the chocolate sets, about 15-20 minutes.

5. Unveil these frozen treats and watch as they disappear quicker than you can say "banana pop!"

Ingredients

- 4 large bananas
- 2 cups gluten-free dark or milk chocolate chips
- 1 tablespoon coconut oil
- Toppings: crushed gluten-free cookies, sprinkles, chopped nuts, coconut flakes
- Popsicle sticks or skewers

As we bite into our chocolate-covered creations, the kitchen erupts with laughter and chocolatey smiles. "Papa, this is fruit! So it's healthy" Stella proudly exclaims, while Mia plans out her next banana pop masterpiece. It's moments like these that make the kitchen the heart of our home – a place for creativity, joy, and delicious treats.

IRRESISTIBLE
Chickpea Truffles

Today, we're diving into a delightful creation that combines the unexpected with the delicious. These Chickpea Truffles are a treat you won't be able to resist, and the best part? They're hiding a secret superfood – chickpeas!

As parents, we know the never-ending quest to sneak some extra nutrition into our kids' diets. Chickpeas are packed with protein and nutrients, making them a perfect addition to your little one's meals. But what if I told you that you could get your kids to enjoy chickpeas without them even realizing it?

Let's gather our ingredients and get started:

Prepare Time
10 Minutes

Cool Time
2 hours

Ingredients

- 1 can (13.5oz) of chickpeas, drained and rinsed.
- 1/2 cup of nut or seed butter (I like peanut or almond butter)
- 1 cup of dark chocolate chips, melted

For the Coating:
- 1 cup of vegan dark chocolate chips, melted
- 1 tbsp of coconut oil

Optional Toppings:
- Sprinkles
- Shredded coconut
- Nuts/seeds

Instructions

1. Let's kick things off by giving those chickpeas a good rinse and drain. Next, melt the dark chocolate in the microwave or stovetop.

2. Now, it's blending time! In your trusty food processor, add the chickpeas, nut butter, and those velvety melted chocolate chips. Blend away for about 45-60 seconds, or until everything is beautifully incorporated.

3. With a ice-cream scoop, roll them into balls and drop them onto a baking sheet lined with parchment paper. Pop these little wonders into the freezer for about 15-20 minutes to firm up.

4. While your truffles are in their final chill, let's get the chocolate coating ready. Melt another batch of dark chocolate and coconut oil – we're going all-in with that chocolatey goodness.

5. Take the truffles out of the freezer and give them a nice, cozy chocolate bath. Then, place them back on the parchment paper-lined baking sheet and back into the freezer to achieve ultimate firmness.

6. If you're feeling fancy, this is where you can sprinkle on some of those optional toppings. Get creative and make each truffle a unique masterpiece.

7. And there you have it, your Chickpea Truffles are ready to shine. Take them out of the freezer and store them in the fridge.

8. For optimal freshness, savour these delectable bites within 7-10 days if they reside in your fridge or 30-60 days if you prefer to keep them frozen.

Get ready to surprise your taste buds with these nutritious delights. Happy truffle-making, my fellow kitchen adventurers!

Chocolate Chickpeas

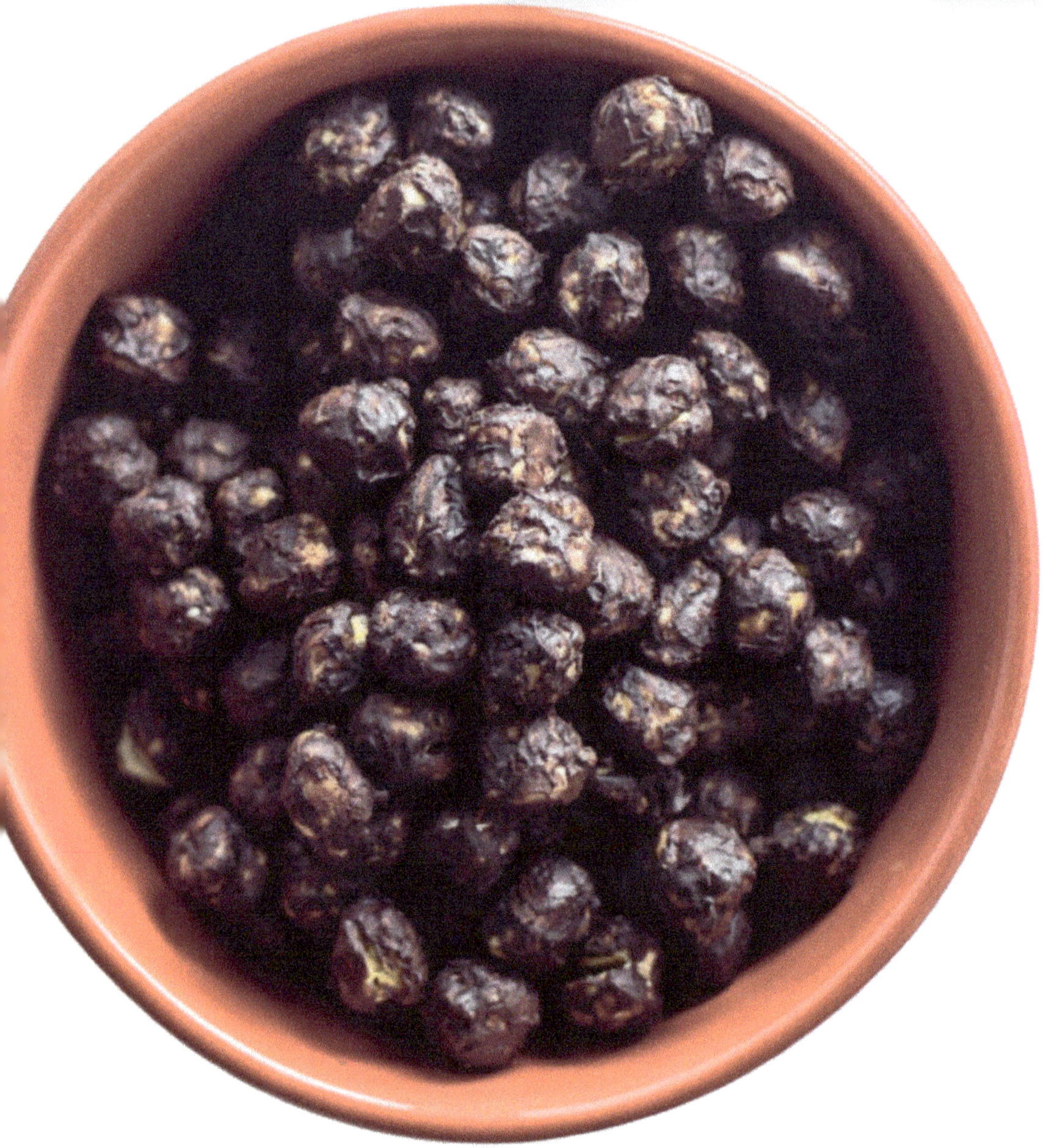

Prepare Time
5 Minutes

Bake Time
30 Minutes

Snacking never felt this good. Looking for a guilt-free, protein-packed snack that your kids will adore? These Chocolate Chickpeas are like a healthy version of M&M's, providing the same delightful chocolatey crunch but without any of the guilt. With just a few simple ingredients and a bit of creativity, you can whip up a snack that's both nutritious and kid-friendly.

Ingredients

- 15 oz. chickpeas, drained, rinsed, and patted dry
- 1 tablespoon coconut oil, melted

For the chocolate:
- ½ cup chocolate chips
- 1 tablespoon coconut oil
- Sea salt

Instructions

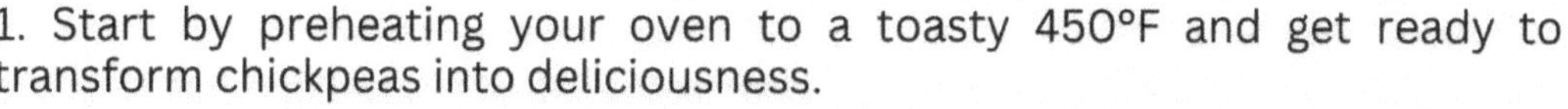

1. Start by preheating your oven to a toasty 450°F and get ready to transform chickpeas into deliciousness.

2. Pour the chickpeas into a mesh strainer to give them a good drain, then rinse them thoroughly. Afterward, transfer these little wonders to a plate and pat them dry gently using a few paper towels.

3. Now, let's get those chickpeas coated to perfection. Place them in a bowl and drizzle the melted coconut oil over them. Give them a good stir until they're evenly coated. Then, transfer the chickpeas onto a baking sheet lined with parchment paper and pop them into the preheated oven. Roast them for 25-30 minutes, making sure to give them a toss halfway through.

4. While the chickpeas are getting all crispy and delicious in the oven, it's time to work on the chocolatey goodness. Melt the chocolate chips and coconut oil together. You can do this either in a saucepan on the stove or in the microwave, just make sure to stir frequently until the chocolate turns into a smooth, tempting pool of goodness. Pour it into a large bowl.

5. When the chickpeas are all roasted to perfection, transfer them into the bowl with the melted chocolate. Gently stir them to ensure they're evenly coated in that luscious chocolate.

6. Now, spread these chocolate-drenched chickpeas back out onto the baking sheet, sprinkle them with a pinch of sea salt, and place the sheet in the freezer for at least 30 minutes to let that chocolate set.

Once the chocolate has transformed into a delightful, crunchy shell, it's time to enjoy! You can easily break the chocolate chickpeas apart; they won't stick to the pan. And voilà, you have a high-protein, kid-friendly snack that tastes just like M&M's but is so much better for you.

CHICKPEA Cookie Dough

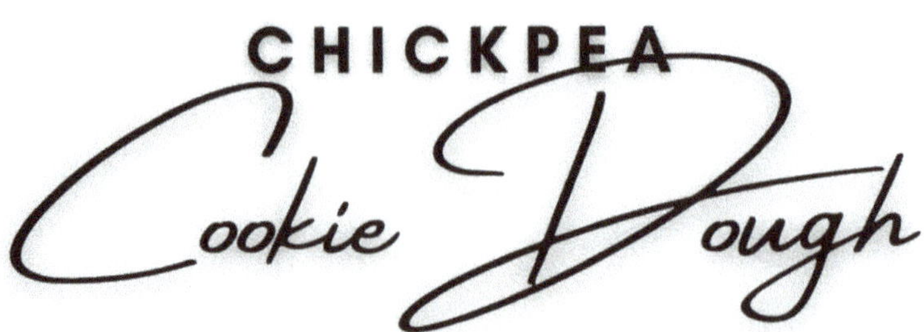

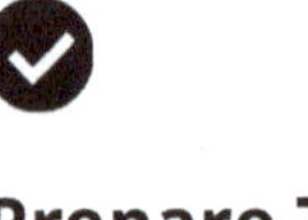

Prepare Time
5 Minutes

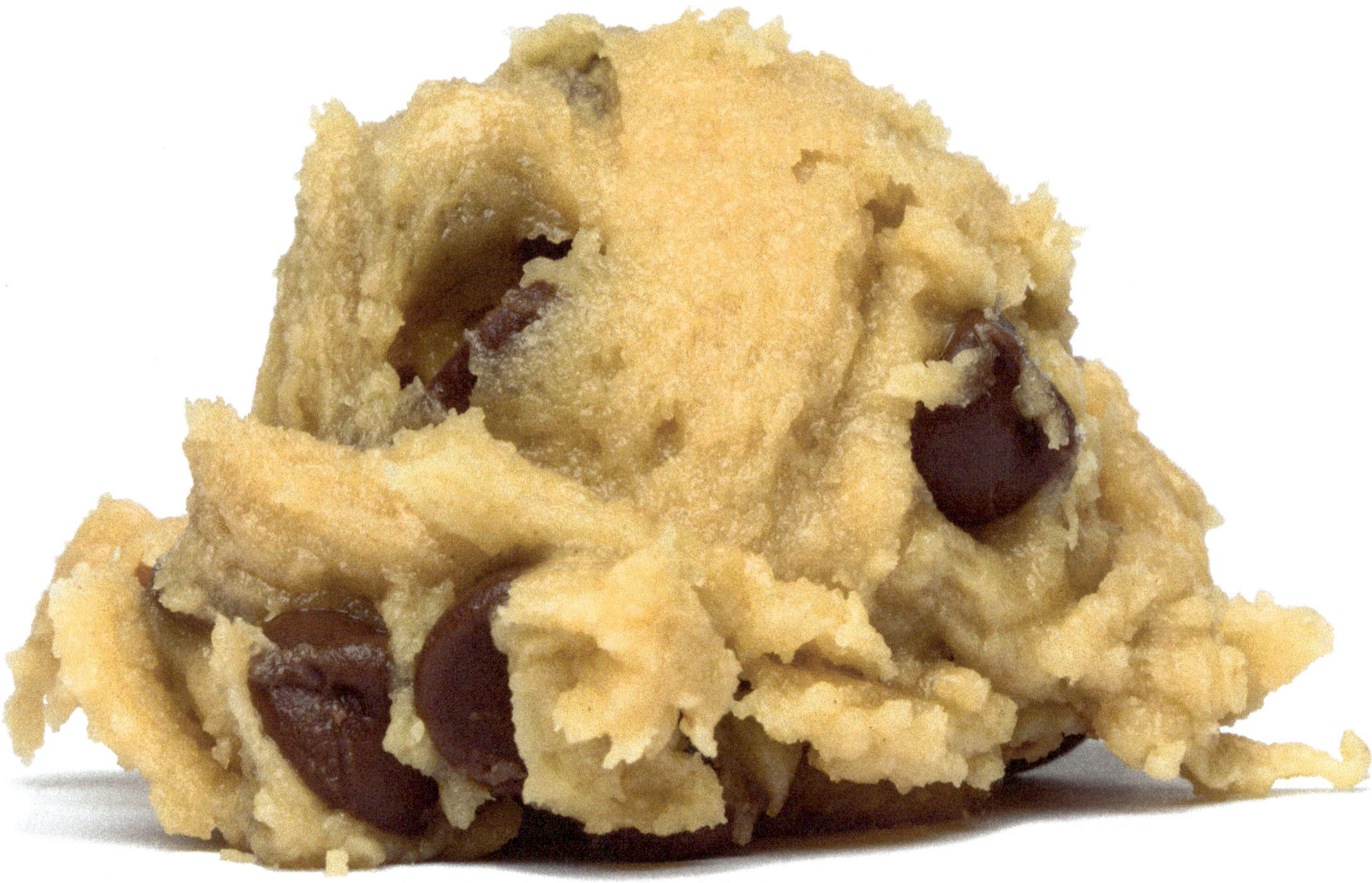

Indulge in a delightful, guilt-free treat with this Chickpea Cookie Dough recipe. Made from a handful of wholesome ingredients, it's a breeze to whip up and oh-so-chocolatey. Let's create a delectable dessert that's both healthy and satisfying.

Ingredients

- 15 oz. chickpeas, drained and rinsed
- 1/4 cup almond flour
- 1/4 cup peanut butter
- 1/2 tsp baking powder
- 1/4 tsp salt
- 1/4 tsp cinnamon (optional)
- 3 tbsp maple syrup
- 1 tsp vanilla extract
- 1/3 cup chocolate chips

Instructions

1. Gather your chickpeas, almond flour, nut butter, baking powder, salt, and cinnamon (if you choose to use it). Throw them into your food processor and give them a whirl for about 10-15 seconds.

2. While the food processor is still running, pour in the syrup and vanilla through the top. This should help the mixture come together and form into cookie dough. You might need to scrape down the sides of the processor once or twice. If it's still not quite there, you can add a teaspoon of milk to help it along.

3. Scoop out your delicious cookie dough into a bowl, and now it's time to add the finishing touch - those chocolate chips. Stir them in and get ready to enjoy!

This Chickpea Cookie Dough is a quick and easy way to satisfy your sweet tooth with healthy ingredients. Plus, it's super fun to make and even more enjoyable to devour!

BIRTHDAY CAKE
cookie dough energy bites

Prepare Time
10 Minutes

Freeze Time
30 Minutes

Serves
8

Make snack time feel like a celebration with these no-bake birthday cake cookie dough energy bites. They're a delicious, kid-friendly treat that tastes just like cake batter! With seven simple ingredients and a burst of festive sprinkles, these vegan energy bites are naturally sweetened with pure maple syrup. They're the perfect protein-packed snack for your little ones.

Ingredients

- 1/2 cup cashew butter (roasted cashews + salt)
- 3 tbsp pure maple syrup
- 1 tsp vanilla extract
- 1/4 tsp almond extract
- 1/3 cup packed fine blanched almond flour
- 1/4 cup flaxseed meal (plus an additional tablespoon if needed)
- 2 tbsp sprinkles
- Extra sprinkles, for rolling

Instructions

1. In a medium bowl, combine cashew butter, pure maple syrup, and vanilla and almond extracts. Mix with a spatula until the mixture is well combined and smooth.

2. Add in the almond flour and flaxseed meal. Mix thoroughly until the ingredients come together, forming a dough. If the dough is too wet, incorporate another tablespoon or two of almond flour or flaxseed meal. Finally, gently fold in the sprinkles.

3. Use a medium cookie scoop to portion the dough and roll it into balls. You should end up with approximately 8 balls. If you wish, roll each ball in additional sprinkles for that extra celebratory touch.

4. Place the energy bites on a baking sheet lined with parchment paper and pop them in the freezer for about 30 minutes until they firm up. Once they've set a bit, you can transfer them to an airtight container and store them in the freezer for up to 3 months. You can enjoy these bites straight from the freezer, or if they're too firm, let them sit at room temperature for 5-10 minutes.

These birthday cake cookie dough energy bites are a delightful way to bring a touch of celebration to snack time. They're a hit with the girls and Frank!

HONEY CINNAMON
almond butter energy bites

Get ready for a burst of deliciousness with these honey cinnamon almond butter energy bites that taste remarkably like cinnamon teddy grahams! These almond butter energy bites are not only easy to make but also packed with fibre and protein. They're made without oats and feature creamy almond butter, flaxseed meal, chia seeds, and your favourite protein powder. This no-bake snack is perfect for a quick energy boost.

Prepare Time
15 Minutes

Cool Time
15 Minutes

Serves
8

Ingredients

- 1/2 cup natural, creamy, drippy almond butter
- 3 tbsp honey
- 1 tsp vanilla
- 1 tsp cinnamon
- 1/2 cup flaxseed meal
- 1 tbsp chia seeds
- 1/4 cup protein powder of your choice
- 2 tbsp chocolate chips
- Sea salt, for sprinkling

Instructions

1. In a medium bowl, combine almond butter, honey, vanilla, and cinnamon. Mix until all the ingredients are well combined.

2. Add flaxseed meal, chia seeds, your choice of protein powder, and mini chocolate chips to the mixture. At this point, you may find it easiest to use your hands to work the dough, ensuring everything is thoroughly mixed. You should be able to form balls that stick together. Depending on the consistency of your nut butter and the protein powder used, you may need to add more nut butter or sweetener to help the balls hold together.

3. Roll the dough into 8 balls and place them on a plate. Sprinkle a touch of sea salt over them for that perfect balance of flavours. Transfer the bites to the fridge to firm up. After about 15 minutes, they should be ready to go. Once firm, you can store them in an airtight container in the fridge for up to 1 week.

These honey cinnamon almond butter energy bites are a delightful combination of flavour and nutrition, making for a satisfying and convenient snack.

It was one of those Saturdays that screamed for a fun kitchen experiment. Armed with a recipe for 5-Minute Protein Peanut Butter Energy Bites that I found online, I decided it was high time to introduce my dynamic duo, Stella and Mia, to the wonders of semi-healthy snacking. "Kids, today we're making what I like to call, 'Papa's Little Helpers' because, frankly, I need all the energy I can get with you two," I announced with a flourish, unveiling the ingredients like a game show host.

Mia squinted at the peanut butter and oats. "Are these like cookies?" she asked hopefully. "Better," I said. "They're like cookies that can bench press."

Stella, always the skeptic, eyed the flax seeds. "Does it have to have that?" she questioned as if I'd just suggested adding broccoli.

"Trust me, you won't even taste it," I assured her, hiding my fingers crossed behind my back.

We started by mixing the oats and peanut butter. "You have to mix it like you're making a potion," I instructed, stirring dramatically. Stella, ever the literalist, began chanting nonsense words over the bowl like a tiny, overzealous witch. "Oatabra Cadabutter!"

Things took a hilarious turn when I handed over the honey. "Squeeze gently," I advised. Apparently, in twin language, 'gently' translates to 'as hard as humanly possible.' Honey oozed over the rim of the bowl like a slow-moving lava flow, pooling onto the counter with a sticky sheen. "It's a honey volcano!" Mia cheered, utterly delighted by the chaos.

"Now, we roll them into balls," I said, moving us on before we ended up with a new kitchen floor made of honey. This was where the real fun began. Stella, with hands gooey from the mixture, decided now was the perfect time to decorate my face with oatmeal spots. "Look, Papa, you're an oatmeal monster!"

Meanwhile, Mia, a budding perfectionist, rolled each bite as precisely as a master jeweller, critiquing the roundness of each sphere like it was a diamond. "This one's more like a triangle," she frowned, squishing it between her fingers and starting over.

Several sticky, gooey, hilariously misshapen protein bites later, we surveyed our work with pride. They were uneven, overly honeyed, and probably more glittery than necessary (thanks to a last-minute addition by Stella, who couldn't resist), but they were ours.

"We did it!" Mia exclaimed, holding up a particularly globby bite as if it were a trophy.

"Yeah," I agreed, popping one into my mouth and instantly regretting the generous amount of honey. "We definitely did something."

As we sat there, munching on our creations, I realized that these kitchen capers with my girls weren't just about making snacks. They were about making memories—sticky, messy, wonderfully sweet memories. And maybe, just maybe, that made them the best kind of cookies... or whatever these were supposed to be.

5-MINUTE PROTEIN
peanut butter energy bites

Prepare Time
5 Minutes

Cool Time
5 Minutes

Serves
10

Let me take you back to the first time I tried these incredible no-bake protein-packed peanut butter energy bites. It was during a hiking trip in the Alps. As I reached the top, a fellow hiker offered me one of these little bites, and it was like a burst of energy. I knew I had to recreate them. Now, I'm thrilled to share these chewy, peanut butter cookie dough-flavoured energy bites that are not only delicious but also loaded with wholesome ingredients like flaxseed, chia, and oats. They've become a staple in our family for quick, healthy snacks.

Ingredients

- 1/2 cup natural, drippy peanut butter
- 1/4 cup honey (or date syrup or coconut syrup)
- 1 teaspoon vanilla extract
- 1/3 cup protein powder of your choice*
- 1/3 cup flaxseed meal
- 1/2 cup rolled GF oats
- 1/2 teaspoon cinnamon
- 1 tablespoon chia seeds
- 1 tablespoon mini chocolate chips (vegan, if desired)
- 1/4 cup unsweetened shredded coconut

Instructions

1. In the bowl of a food processor, combine the peanut butter, honey, vanilla, protein powder, flaxseed meal, oats, cinnamon, and chia seeds. Pulse everything together until it's well combined. Then, add in the chocolate chips (and coconut if you're using it) and pulse a few more times.

2. Use a medium cookie scoop or your hands to grab the dough and roll it into 10 equally-sized balls. Place these bites in an airtight container.

To make without a food processor: Add the wet ingredients to a medium bowl and mix them to combine. Then, add in the dry ingredients and mix until everything comes together. It's usually at this point that I find myself digging in with my hands to ensure the dough is perfectly mixed. You should be able to form balls that stick together. Remember, the consistency of peanut butter can vary, so depending on what type of protein powder you use, you may need to adjust the amount of nut butter or sweetener to help the balls stick together.

3. Store your peanut butter energy bites in the fridge for up to 1 week, or in the freezer for up to 2 months. They're a quick, nutritious, and utterly satisfying snack to enjoy anytime, whether you're on a hiking adventure or just need a pick-me-up during your busy day.

These energy bites are a delightful reminder of that memorable time and a testament to the power of good food to fuel our journeys.

Who says cookies need to be baked? Let's toss that rule out the window with something I like to call "Apple Cookie Crunchers." Imagine this: it's snack time, the kids are climbing the walls, and you've got exactly five minutes to whip up something before the youngins stage a mutiny. Enter the superhero snack that's quick, delicious, and has at least one fruit in it, so you can feel like a responsible parent.

Ingredients

- 1 apple – because we're making cookies, but let's keep the doctor away too.
- ¼ cup peanut butter – the glue of the snack world.
- ¼ cup sliced almonds – for that crunch.
- ¼ cup chopped walnuts – more crunch, because why not?
- ¼ cup shredded coconut – it's like tropical snow.
- ¼ cup chocolate chips – because chocolate. Enough said.

Instructions

1. Start by slicing your apple into thin rings. Yes, thin. We're not making apple steaks here. Oh, and get rid of the core unless you've got a thing for apple seeds.

2. Grab a knife—or your fingers, I'm not judging—and slather a generous layer of peanut butter on one side of each apple ring. This is where it gets messy, but hey, that's half the fun, right?

3. Now for the art project part. Sprinkle those rings with almonds, walnuts, coconut, and a liberal scattering of chocolate chips. Go wild. Make it rain chocolate chips if you want. This is your circus.

4. That's it. No baking, no waiting. Just straight to the serving plate and watch them disappear faster than your chance to sit down.

And there you go—"Apple Cookie Crunchers." Quick, easy, and suspiciously healthy (thanks to the apple, not the chocolate chips). Perfect for when you need a quick fix to keep the peace and give the kids (and yourself) a treat. Whip these up, bask in the glory of your culinary genius, and keep those tiny rebels happy. Here's to snacks that save the day!

OLD-FASHIONED Gingerbread Bundt Cake

As soon as the holidays roll around, our household transforms into a gingerbread factory. There's flour flying everywhere and sticky fingers smearing batter all over the counters. But it's worth it for the Old-Fashioned Gingerbread Bundt Cake, a legendary treat that my girls love. And let's be real, anything that doesn't require too much effort is a win.

Ingredients

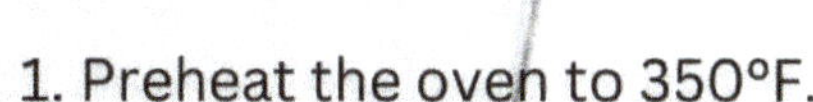

Instructions

For the cake:

- ¾ cup (163 g) Dark Brown Sugar, packed
- 1 tbsp (6 g) orange zest, finely grated
- 2¾ cups (344 g) all-purpose gluten-free flour
- 2 tsp Xanthan gum (if flour doesn't already have it)
- 1 tbsp (5 g) ground ginger
- 2 tsp (6 g) ground cinnamon
- 1½ tsp (7 g) baking soda
- ½ tsp (3 g) salt
- ½ tsp (1 g) ground cloves
- ½ tsp (1 g) ground nutmeg
- ¾ cup (170 g) butter
- 1 egg
- ¾ cup (188 ml) unsulfured or fancy molasses (do not use blackstrap molasses)
- 1 cup (250 ml) boiling water

For the glaze:

- 1 cup (120 g) Icing Sugar
- 2 tbsp (28 g) butter, melted and slightly cooled
- 1 tbsp (15 ml) milk
- 2 tsp (10 ml) pure vanilla extract
- ¼ tsp (2 g) salt

1. Preheat the oven to 350°F.

2. Brush a 9- or 10-inch bundt pan with a thin, even layer of neutral oil or shortening. Make sure to grease all surfaces, especially if using an intricately detailed bundt pan. Dust the pan with a coating of flour, ensuring even coverage.

3. Combine Redpath® Dark Brown Sugar with orange zest, massaging them together until the orange zest releases its aromatic oils. Set aside.

4. In a large bowl, whisk together the gluten-free flour, ginger, cinnamon, baking soda, salt, cloves, and nutmeg.

5. In a stand mixer or using a hand mixer, cream the butter and the brown sugar mixture until pale and fluffy. Add the egg and mix until fully incorporated. Mix in the molasses.

6. Gradually add a third of the dry ingredients to the batter, alternating with hot water. Mix until just combined, being careful not to overmix.

7. Transfer the batter into the prepared bundt pan, placing it on a baking sheet for stability. Bake for 40 to 45 minutes, or until a skewer inserted comes out clean and the top springs back when gently pressed.

8. Allow the cake to cool in the pan for 10 minutes. Gently tap the sides and shake the pan to loosen the cake. If needed, gently pull the edges away. Invert the pan onto a serving dish, letting the cake release itself.

9. In a separate bowl, whisk together Redpath® Icing Sugar, melted butter, milk, vanilla extract, and salt. Pour the glaze over the cooled cake, letting it elegantly drip down the sides.

10. Garnish the cake with orange zest, cranberries, candied ginger, or herbs before the glaze sets.

11. Store any leftovers in an airtight container at room temperature for up to 3 days or in the fridge for a week.

This Old-Fashioned Gingerbread Bundt Cake has become more than a recipe; it's a cherished part of our holiday celebration, bringing warmth and joy to our family gatherings. May it do the same for yours!

CRISPY BAKED
Kale Chips

Snack time just got a whole lot healthier and more delicious! When you're in the mood for a crunchy, guilt-free snack, these Crispy Baked Kale Chips are the perfect solution. Made from fresh Tuscan kale leaves and seasoned with a hint of olive oil, sea salt, and onion powder, these chips offer a delightful combination of flavours and textures. Whether you're looking for a quick and healthy treat or a satisfying side, these kale chips will have your taste buds dancing with every bite.

Prepare Time
5 Minutes

Bake Time
30 Minutes

Ingredients

- 1 bunch Tuscan kale
- ½ tablespoon olive oil
- Heaping ⅛ teaspoon fine sea or kosher salt
- ¼ teaspoon onion powder

Instructions

1. Start by preheating your oven to a toasty 275 degrees Fahrenheit.

2. Begin by washing the kale leaves and then pat them dry thoroughly with a clean dish towel. Once they're dry, tear the kale leaves away from the stems and shape them into the desired chip-sized pieces. In a medium-sized bowl, gently toss the kale leaves with a touch of olive oil, ensuring they're evenly coated.

3. Line a baking sheet with parchment paper to prevent any sticking. Place the kale leaves in a single layer on the prepared sheet and sprinkle them with just the right amount of sea salt and onion powder.

4. It's time to bake these little green wonders! Pop them in the preheated oven and let them bake for 30 to 35 minutes until the kale leaves turn perfectly crisp.

5. Once they're done, let them cool for a moment, and then dig in! These kale chips are at their best when enjoyed immediately. But if, by some miracle, you have leftovers, you can store them in a sealed container for up to one day.

There you have it – a simple, healthy, and utterly satisfying snack that everyone in your family will love. With a fantastic combination of crispy texture and delectable flavour, these Crispy Baked Kale Chips are sure to become a household favourite in no time

ROASTED
Chickpeas

Prepare Time
10 Minutes

Bake Time
25 Minutes

Serves
4-6

Get ready to embark on a crunchy adventure – our destination? Roasted Chickpeas, a snack that is both nutritious and satisfyingly crispy. Let me be your guide as we transform these simple yet versatile legumes into a delicious snack. This is the perfect option for an after-school treat, and it's significantly healthier than traditional chips.

- 2 cans (15 oz each) chickpeas, drained and rinsed
- 2 tablespoons olive oil
- 1 teaspoon smoked paprika
- 1/2 teaspoon garlic powder
- 1/2 teaspoon onion powder
- Salt to taste
- Optional: pinch of cayenne pepper or chili powder for a kick

Instructions

1. Begin your adventure by drying the chickpeas thoroughly with a towel. This is key to achieving that perfect crunch!

2. In a bowl, toss the chickpeas with olive oil, smoked paprika, garlic powder, onion powder, and a generous pinch of salt. If the family's feeling bold, add that optional pinch of cayenne or chili powder.

3. Spread the chickpeas on a baking sheet in a single layer. Roast them in the oven at 400°F (200°C) for 20-25 minutes, or until they're golden and crispy. Give them a stir halfway through for even crunchiness.

4. Let the chickpeas cool slightly – they'll get even crunchier as they cool down. This is the hardest part, waiting for the crunchy goodness!

5. Gather the family and dive into your bowl of roasted chickpeas. It's a crunch-fest that even the crispiest potato chips would envy!

As the last chickpea is crunched, Mia and Stella look up with satisfied smiles, their fingers tinged with paprika and salt. "Papa, can we make these for every snack?" they ask, already planning their next chickpea flavor experiments. And just like that, a new family-favorite snack is born. Here's to healthy munching, crunching, and creating joyful memories – one chickpea at a time!

CRISPY *Veggie Chips*

Prepare Time
15 Minutes

Bake Time
25 Minutes

Serves
4-6

Get ready to embark on a crunchy adventure – our As a parent, I know how difficult it can be to get kids to eat their vegetables. That's why I've taken on the challenge of creating a crispy and tasty garden adventure by turning ordinary veggies into delightful Veggie Chips. Join me on this journey where veggies take center stage during snack time. Prepare yourself for some satisfying crunches, joyful giggles, and a whole lot of fun. Watch as your children fall in love with vegetables transformed into irresistible chips. It's a healthy twist on a crunchy experience!

- A selection of root vegetables (such as sweet potatoes, beets, carrots, and parsnips)
- 2 tablespoons olive oil
- Sea salt, to taste
- Optional seasonings: garlic powder, rosemary, thyme, or smoked paprika

Instructions

1. Start your voyage by thinly slicing your chosen veggies. A mandoline slicer is perfect for getting those ultra-thin, crisp slices. Let Mia and Stella pick their favourite veggies to slice (with a little help, of course).

2. Toss the slices in olive oil and a sprinkle of sea salt. If you're feeling adventurous, add a dash of your favourite seasonings. Maybe garlic powder for an extra kick or rosemary for a herby touch.

3. Lay the slices out on a baking sheet lined with parchment paper, making sure they don't overlap. Bake them in a preheated oven at 375°F (190°C) for 20-25 minutes or until they're crispy and golden. Flip them halfway through for even crunching.

4. Allow the chips to cool on the baking sheet. They'll get even crispier as they cool – if you can wait that long!

5. Gather the family and dive into your homemade veggie chips. Watch as even the most veggie-skeptical eyes light up at the first crunchy bite.

The girls exchange amazed glances as they finish off the last crunchy veggie chip. "We made these from real vegetables?" they exclaim, already planning their next vegetable chip experiment. We've turned a healthy snack into a fun and delicious family activity. Here's to turning vegetables into irresistible treats and showing that nutritious can also mean tasty!

Savoring the Gluten-Free Journey

Ah, my dear reader, here we are at the end of our delicious journey, and damn, it's been one hell of a ride. Thanks a million for letting me crash into your kitchen, your home, and, let's be honest, probably a bit of your sanity. We've whipped up some truly kick-ass, kid-friendly, gluten-free dishes that'll go down in family history.

Parenting? It's like being the ringmaster of your own personal circus. Seriously, it's like juggling flaming chainsaws while blindfolded on a high wire. Amid this delightful chaos, we crave simple, tasty, and somewhat nutritious meals that don't take a lifetime to make.

This cookbook became your secret weapon—a beacon of hope in the stormy seas of family meal prep. It's filled with recipes that aren't just about filling bellies, but about creating those unforgettable, "please don't grow up too fast" moments.

Remember those pancake breakfasts where batter became abstract art and syrup ended up in unimaginable places? That wasn't just breakfast; it was a launchpad for their day. And those dinner triumphs—the times your kids paused mid-bite to declare, "This is the best ever!"—those were the meals that turned "just dinner" into a victory parade.

Oh, and the late-night snack raids? Legendary. Those sneakily sweet moments will be what you look back on laughing when the kids are out building their own lives. Cooking is more than just throwing ingredients together; it's how we say "I love you," "I got you," and "Yes, you can have dessert" without uttering a word. Every dish you serve up is a hug, a high-five, a celebration of being together.

So, let's get real about this whole gluten-free thing—it wasn't a trendy lifestyle choice for me; it was an absolute must. My body basically said, "Enough with the gluten, buddy," and the change was like night and day. It felt like I'd solved a puzzle that had been messing with me for years. Going gluten-free wasn't just about nixing a few ingredients; it was about opening a door to new flavors, funky grains, and dishes I thought I'd have to give up forever. The real win? Watching my family thrive—more energy, better digestion, just feeling damn good.

That's what fired me up to create Gluten-Free Family Adventures . Think of it as your go-to for gluten-free meals that don't skimp on flavour or fun. It's packed with everything from slammin' breakfasts to killer desserts, making sure everyone at your table leaves happy.

As we wrap this up, come follow me on Instagram @thedaddiaries.ca. It's the perfect spot to keep swapping recipes, tips, and tales from our parenting trenches—all while keeping the foodie fun alive.

To you, the unsung kitchen heroes: hats off. You juggle breakfast, break up fights, and bang out emails simultaneously. You turn the everyday into something epic. Every meal you make is a memory in the making.

Thanks for letting me tag along on your crazy culinary journey. Until we meet again, keep savoring every bite, treasuring every moment, and keep those oven mitts ready.

Here's to staying messy, cheesy, and just a little bit greasy.

Joseph Tito.

Follow Along

thedaddiaries.com

 @thedaddiaries.ca    @thedaddiaries    @thedaddiaries